W9-BET-370

THREADBEAR

A story of Christian healing
for adult survivors of sexual abuse

by **Tilda Norberg**

Art and book design
by **Joyce Thomas**

PENN HOUSE PRESS, NY

Library of Congress
Catalog Card Number
97-67581

Norberg, Tilda
Thomas, Joyce

ISBN 0-9658707-0-7

For all the "grown-up little girls"
who shared their healing journeys

and for

Shana Norberg-McClain
and Noah Norberg-McClain.

ACKNOWLEDGEMENT

We are profoundly grateful for the many survivors whose stories are combined in this book.

We want to thank those who encouraged this project from the beginning, especially members of the Prayer House Community, who nudged, supported, and prayed.

Special thanks to Rev. Wanda Craner, Rev. Sara Goold and Daniel Williams for so generously lending their support, expertise and enthusiasm every step of the way.

Please read the

INTRODUCTION

before you read the story.

■

Perhaps you picked up this book because you know or suspect you have been sexually abused as a child. If so, you may feel hopeless about ever feeling better. You may be very angry at your abuser or at God. You may be afraid or ashamed. You may be numb. All these feelings are normal.

I am an ordained United Methodist minister and a Gestalt Pastoral Psychotherapist. I have been working with survivors of sexual abuse for the past 25 years. I know from experience that with healing prayer — and some hard work — the terrible pain of childhood sexual abuse can be healed.

Threadbear is a composite story about the process of healing from sexual abuse for a Christian. It is based on the stories of many brave and wonderful survivors who have faced their memories and have been healed by God. Although each person's journey will be unique, the movements toward wholeness often echo that of the "grown-up little girl" of *Threadbear*.

Many survivors of sexual abuse feel utterly abandoned by God, bewildered about why God would allow such horrors, and are angry at God for not having prevented them. Each survivor needs to find answers to these questions which satisfy her heart.

The "grown-up little girl" of the story finds her answers — as well as her memories — in Threadbear, a stuffed animal of her childhood. She, like so many adult survivors of abuse, recalls that her only comfort as a child was found in a soft animal toy.

I have come to believe that an anguished Christ who weeps with the suffering children also finds a way to express his love for them. Sometimes — quite often — this love of God for a lonely, frightened child is embodied in a lowly teddy bear. For persons of faith, an important part of recovery is discovering for themselves this healing action of God.

The approach described in *Threadbear* is that of Gestalt Pastoral Care, a combination of Gestalt psychotherapy, spiritual companioning, and a special kind of healing prayer called "faith imagination." Faith imagination is a way of inviting Jesus' healing love to transform pain. This way of praying asks God to use your capacity for imaginative attention so you can perceive how God's grace is healing you.

Most people find it much easier to re-live a painful or terrifying memory when they know they don't have to go back there all alone. Having Jesus present with them in the memory can make all the difference. Although we can never predict how God will work,

I have come to expect God to act powerfully when we allow God to enter our lives in this way.

You may not imagine Jesus with visual images like the "grown-up little girl" of the story. Some don't "see" images at all when they pray. That's okay. Maybe you will "hear" words, or just have a feeling of God's presence. Maybe you will receive a new idea about the past that puts everything in a new context. There is no right way to pray with faith imagination except in the way that's natural for you.

Some abuse survivors feel scared of almost every man, including Jesus. If you are afraid of Jesus right now or just don't like his maleness, don't worry. Our faith has many wonderful symbols for God through which healing can come. You might try inviting into your memories:

the Holy Spirit,

or Mary, the mother of Jesus,

or Light,

or God's Love,

or God your Rock and Fortress,

or Angel warriors and guardians.

You may find that you are ready to trust Jesus more as healing comes. For now, pray in whatever way you can, knowing that God loves you as you are. You may have some strong emotions as you read *Threadbear*. Remember, you are in control of how much to read at a time. You can take it in small doses if you want. If you are very frightened, it is a good idea to read this book with your therapist. I suggest that before you read any further, you ask God to surface only the feelings or memories you can handle now, and to hold the rest for you until you are ready. Go ahead and pray. Do it now. Really!

If you would like to mute the feelings that do come, ask God or Jesus to seal them up for you until you feel safer. Perhaps you can see or sense this happening as you pray. Try just focusing on what is happening to you right now, this minute. Ask yourself:

What color are the walls, the floor, the chairs in the room where I am reading? What do I see right now that I especially like?

What can I hear right now? A clock ticking? A car going by? A dog barking?

What sensations do I feel right now? A fuzzy rug under my toes? A soft couch with squashy pillows? A cold wet washcloth on my face?

Just being aware of your five senses in the present can help you remember that you are no longer little and helpless. Right now you are safe. It can show you that you can take a peek at a memory or experience a feeling, and then return to the present whenever you want.

I suggest that you not try to complete the journey of healing alone. Find a helper — perhaps a therapist or pastor — who can embody Christ for you, who is a good listener, and who won't judge you. Look for someone who is skilled but not rigid, and who knows the territory from experience. Look for a person who believes that God can heal you, and is willing to pray for that.

I trust that the healing love of God will pour out, nurturing you in just the way you need, empowering you to do the hard work of growing, and loving you into wholeness.

TILDA NORBERG

Chapter I

MANY YEARS AGO

there was a little girl who hid with her bear in the dark closet. She was scared all the time, but when she scrunched down under the clothes and hugged Bear, she felt safer.

"Maybe Daddy won't find me today,"
she would say to herself. And sometimes, if she
was very, very quiet, he didn't. Holding on to
Bear, she learned how to make herself into a
tiny ball. That way she wouldn't cry or scream
or make even a little noise.

Sometimes Daddy was nice, but sometimes
he did bad things to her. She never knew how
he was going to be. Every once in a while,
the bad things felt sort of good . . .

and bad . . .

at the same time.

She wanted him to love her. And hated
it when he did. It made her so mixed up!

She said to herself, "If I'm very, very good,
maybe Daddy will stop." But no matter how
hard she tried,

she could never be good enough,

because

the bad things

kept happening.

Mommy didn't seem

to notice anything at all.

She acted as if

everything was fine.

That made the little
girl even more
mixed up
and lonely.

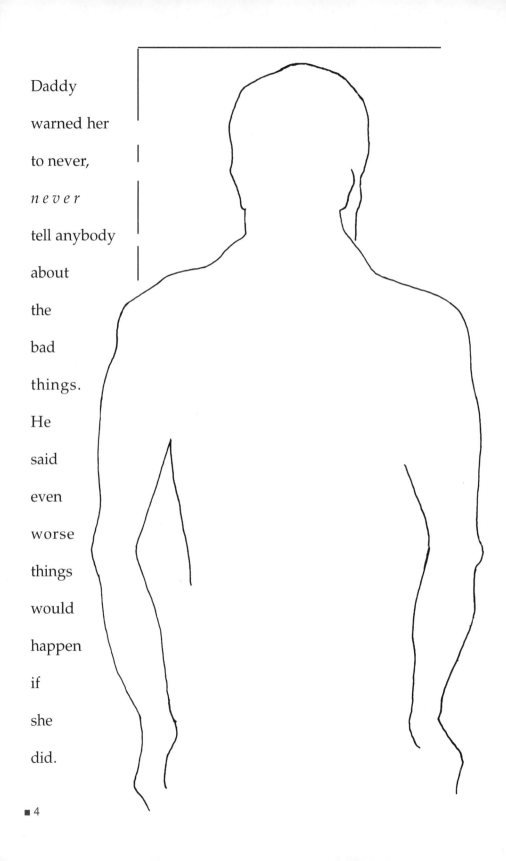

Daddy

warned her

to never,

n e v e r

tell anybody

about

the

bad

things.

He

said

even

worse

things

would

happen

if

she

did.

And so she didn't.

At church,

where her family went every Sunday,

there was a lovely picture of Jesus

holding children on his lap. She would stare

at that picture, longing to be there with the

happy children.

It would be so wonderful

to be snugly and safe with someone.

But then,

Jesus might know

that she was not a very good girl.

He wouldn't like her. And worst of all,

he might do the same bad things to her

that Daddy did.

She had to make herself not notice

the picture anymore.

One day

hiding in the closet

with Bear,

she discovered

she could

speak to Bear

from her heart

without saying

any words at all.

She found

she could tell Bear

all her

terrible secrets.

Bear understood,

and loved her

just the same.

From then on

it was Bear who cried when she didn't dare,

like when the bad things were happening or

when she and Bear were in the closet.

Sometimes Bear was very angry with

Daddy and Mommy.

Sometimes Bear just seemed to say,

"I love you."

That made her feel a little less lonely.

She told Bear everything

without making a single sound.

Bear kept
all her secrets.
And she could forget
and not feel
so bad.

As the years passed,

the little girl got bigger.

She didn't want Bear around

anymore. For some reason she

didn't even want to look at

Bear. So she packed

Bear

away.

Chapter II

At last

the little girl grew into a young woman.

As soon as she could, she left home

to begin a new life.

But something was terribly wrong.

She didn't feel angry or sad or scared.

She didn't feel much of anything at all,

just frozen inside.

She had no close friends. She asked

herself, "Who would want to be with

a person like me?"

She was frightened of lots of things,

and her body was tight and achy.

She tried to tell God about it, but God

seemed far, far away.

She didn't know what was the matter.

She had forgotten all her secrets.

In fact,

she could hardly remember anything at all

about her childhood.

One day

she was in a store,

and saw a lovely, soft bear

sitting on a shelf.

She said to herself, "I want that bear!"

Then pulling herself together tightly

she thought, "How silly. Grown-ups don't need bears."

And she walked out of the store.

But the bear

stayed

in her heart,

tugging at her memory.

A short time later,

something in her began to wake up.

The grown-up began to think about the

frightened little girl

hiding

in the closet.

"Why did I hide in the closet so much?

What was I so afraid of?" she asked herself.

It was not pleasant to remember, but it felt good

in a scary sort of way. The little girl inside finally

felt safe enough to feel again, just a little bit.

She wouldn't plan to remember about the clos-

et, but sometimes the thoughts would just crowd

in. Sometimes she tried to stop the thoughts,

but they kept on coming.

The really-awful-sick-to-her-stomach thought

that didn't even have words yet, was that she

was hiding from . . .

daddy . . .

in the closet.

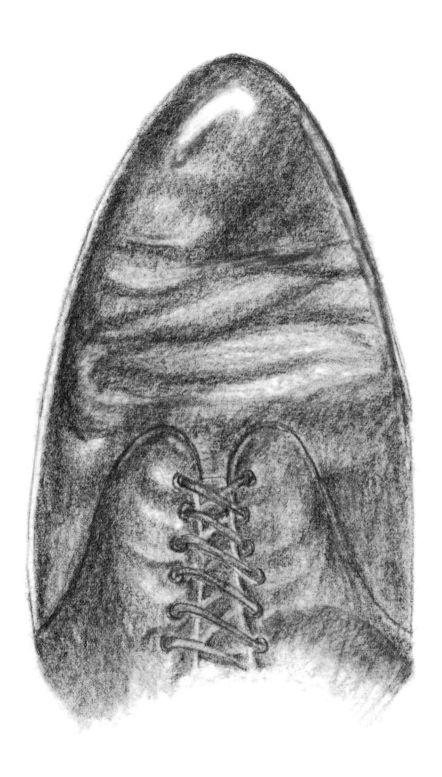

During this time,

she often felt like crying for no reason.

But the tears wouldn't come.

She grouched at bus drivers and store clerks.

It was hard to get out of bed in the morning.

People at work wondered what was wrong.

"AM I GOING CRAZY?" she asked herself.

"AM I GOING *CRAZY?*" she asked God.

But all she heard was

s i l e n c e.

When she couldn't stand it anymore,

she decided to find someone to help.

Chapter III

She found a kind,
understanding person
who had heard many stories like hers.
Someone who was also good
at keeping secrets —— a helper.

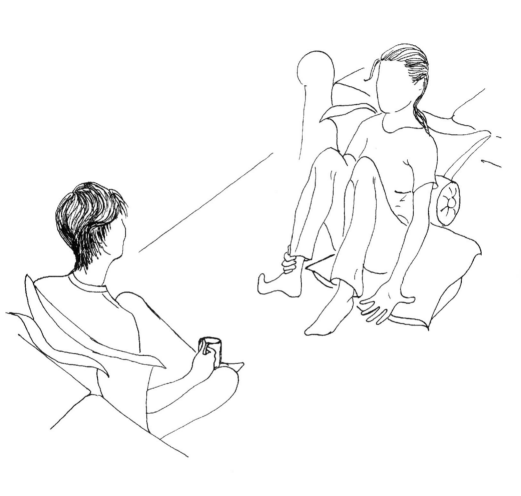

It felt good

to talk to Helper

about

feeling

crazy.

But

she didn't tell

about hiding

in the closet.

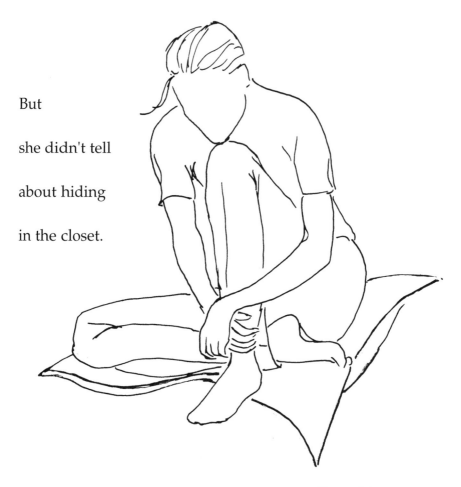

Something

about that closet

was too awful,

and must never, never

be mentioned.

Chapter IV

One day
she was looking in an old trunk
in the attic of the house where she lived
as a little girl. At the very bottom of
the trunk was something soft
wrapped in an old towel.
She pulled it out and found . . .

Bear!

She had not seen Bear for many years.

Gladness bubbled up in her heart.

She knew that Bear belonged to the little girl

in the closet,

and that she wanted to take Bear home

into her grown-up life.

Bear looked very old and tattered.

In fact, Bear's fur was almost worn off.

Remembering

that she had often talked to Bear

when she was little, she exclaimed,

"My, you certainly are threadbare!"

Then smiling to herself,

she said, "and that's what I will call you

from now on,

"THREADBEAR!"

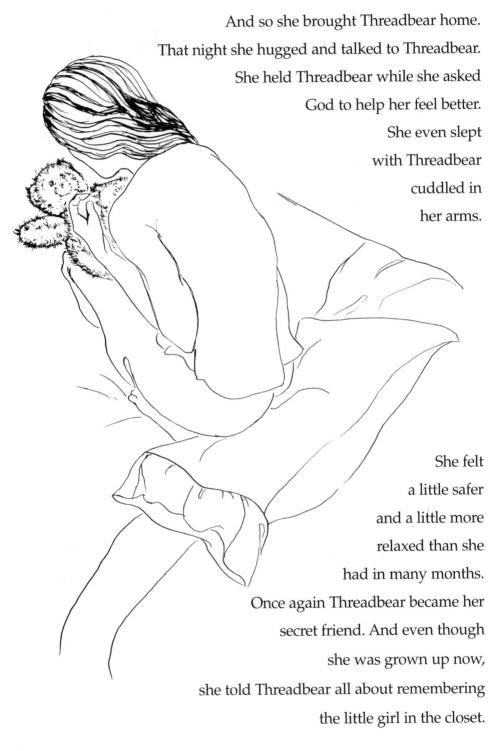

And so she brought Threadbear home.
That night she hugged and talked to Threadbear.
She held Threadbear while she asked
God to help her feel better.
She even slept
with Threadbear
cuddled in
her arms.

She felt
a little safer
and a little more
relaxed than she
had in many months.
Once again Threadbear became her
secret friend. And even though
she was grown up now,
she told Threadbear all about remembering
the little girl in the closet.

Chapter V

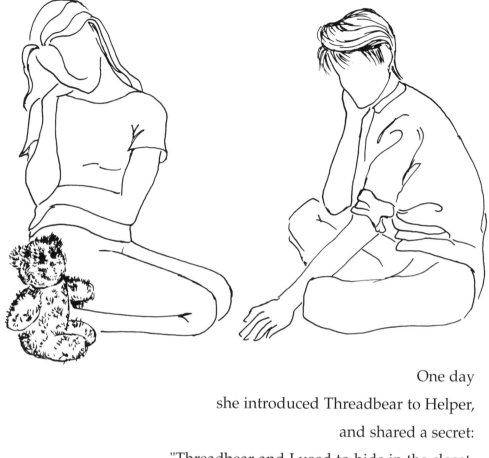

One day

she introduced Threadbear to Helper,

and shared a secret:

"Threadbear and I used to hide in the closet.

I was so scared."

Helper said,

"What was outside the closet that you were hiding from?

What was so scary?"

She held her breath, her heart racing.

Something terrible would happen if she answered.

But Threadbear seemed to whisper:

daddy.

"Daddy,"

she choked.

"I think it's Daddy. I'm scared of Daddy."

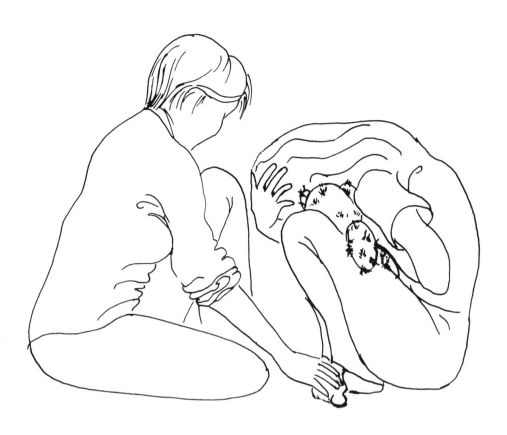

Then she could say no more,

for something icy melted inside, and she cried

for the first time in many years.

Some of the tears that day were almost as old as she

was, and they soaked into what was left of

Threadbear's soft fur.

When the tears were finished, she felt better
for a few minutes. But very soon
she felt terrified.
"Now I'm really going to get in trouble,"
she told Helper.
She was very afraid.
"I must have made that up,"
she said.
"It's not Daddy.
It can't be Daddy!"
"Maybe not," Helper responded,
"but you didn't make up those tears.
Or that fear."
Threadbear seemed to nod in agreement.
For some time,
the grown-up little girl was stuck
in feeling afraid.
Then in being afraid of being afraid.
Then in pushing away any thoughts of Daddy.
"It can't be true
because I don't have any memories.
How can I believe it
if I can't remember what happened?"

But her own body —

and Threadbear —

remembered.

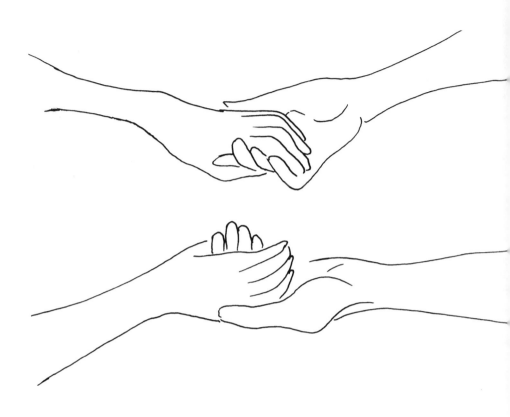

Helper said that Threadbear was rightly named
because Threadbear had given her a "thread" of comfort
to hold on to when she was a child.
In this way she was able to survive.
Threadbear was the keeper of all her tears and anger.
And the bear was the thread that tied the grown-up little
girl to her secrets.
Helper gave thanks for Threadbear
when they prayed.

Chapter VI

There were many times of crying,

and she often held onto

Threadbear, who comforted her

and got wet with her tears.

She was sad for all the years she had lost.

Sad for the terrified little girl.

Sad for the friendless young woman.

Sad. S a d. **Sad.**

Helper would sit with her while she cried,

and together they would pray for more healing.

Then one day Threadbear told her a secret

that she had forgotten long ago. And suddenly

she began to feel things in her body that had

been locked away long before.

Her body,

and then her mind, remembered

Daddy

coming into her room at night

and doing things to her

that no Daddy should ever do

to his child.

Holding her down.

Hurting.

H u r t i n g.

Saying

he would kill her

if she made a sound.

Leaving her there.

Alone. In the dark.

Numb with pain.

And shame.

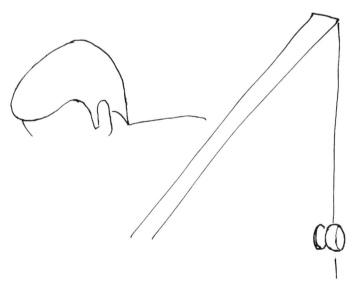

The next day pretending

that nothing

had happened.

Again she thought, "I'm making all this up." But soon she could

almost hear Threadbear—and her own heart—reply

clearly and firmly:

"No. I'm not making it up. It's true. It's all true."

After that,

Threadbear told her more secrets about

what Daddy did,

a little at a time.

It was never easy,

but Threadbear never told her too much

at once.

She was glad she had Helper to steady

and support her.

Chapter VII

Soon

the grown-up girl began to get angry,

very angry.

Angry at Daddy for all the bad, horrible things.

Angry at Mommy for not seeing her misery.

It was frightening to be angry at Mommy

and Daddy, because she had always secretly hoped

that one day they might really love her,

and make everything okay.

Getting angry meant giving up hope . . .

hope that was not really hope at all.

For the first time ever she learned to yell.

In the beginning, she could only squeak.

But soon she learned to make plenty of noise.

She even hit pillows

with her fists, over and over and over again,

to show how angry she was.

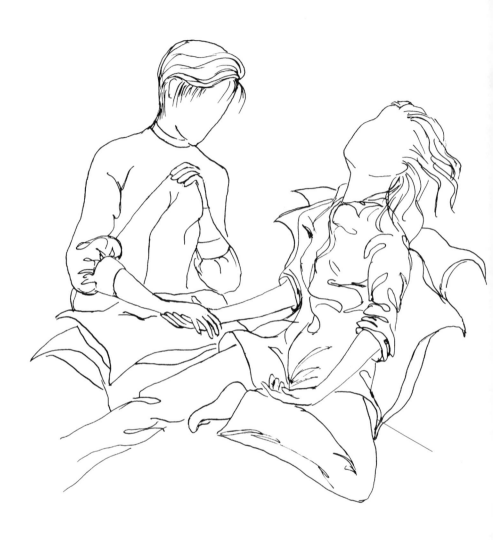

It felt good.

In fact, it felt terrific.

And her body was not so achy any more.

The grown-up little girl

was feeling quite a bit better.

She had gotten back her secrets.

Her tears.

And her anger.

Her body was looser,

and she didn't feel nearly as crazy.

She told Helper

that the truth was setting her free.

Again they thanked God together.

But everything was not all better.

The grown-up little girl found it hard to pray by herself. Prayers felt empty, and they seemed to fall with a thud onto the floor. Unless she was with Helper, God seemed very far away.

"God must feel I'm dirty and unlovable," she would say, even though the grown-up part of her knew better.

She still felt she had somehow caused the bad things, even though she knew that that wasn't really true either.

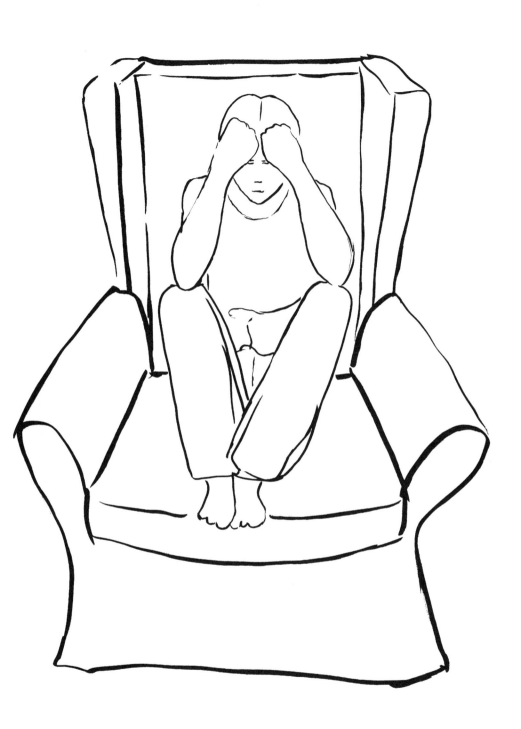

But the little girl inside still felt it.

Chapter VIII

Sometime later,

when she was remembering with Helper,

in her mind she saw the picture

of Jesus and the children.

Right away she found herself yelling at

Jesus from the very center of herself,

a great, big, angry

"Why
was my father so mean?"
she screamed,

"Why
was my mother so blind?"

"Why
didn't you stop him?"

"How could you let him do that to me?"

She picked up a plastic bat and hit the

pillow with a furious WHACK.

"WHERE WERE YOU

when Daddy was coming to my room

every night?"

"WHERE WERE YOU

when he chased me around the house in the

daytime to do bad things to me?"

She paused.

Was it really okay to be furious with

Jesus?

Helper said Jesus could handle it.

Then she sensed that Jesus was there, saying

it was okay to be mad.

"I HATE YOU!"

WHACK!

"YOU DIDN'T DO ANYTHING FOR ME!"

WHACK!

"YOU'RE WEAK!"

WHACK!

"IF YOU LOVE LITTLE CHILDREN, YOU WOULD

NEVER

HAVE LET THIS HAPPEN TO ME!"

"YOU WEREN'T EVEN THERE!"

"YOU DON'T CARE!"

WHACK! WHACK! WHACK!

"WHERE

WERE

YOU?"

wha?

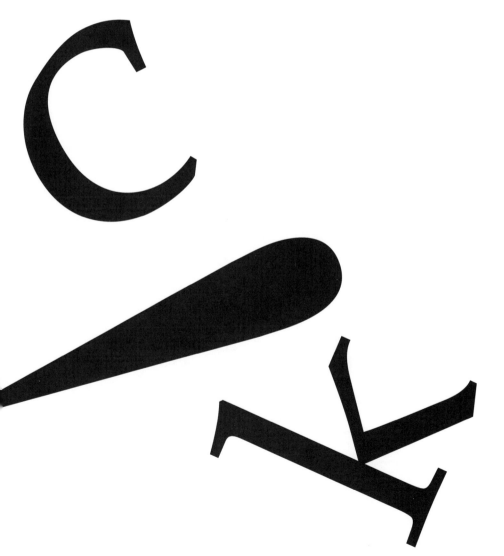

Chapter IX

Finally she stopped,

spent, sweaty, and a little stunned at the

strength of her fury.

She was not feeling angry anymore.

Helper smiled at her and said,

"Go inside and see how Jesus is

responding to you."

So the grown-up little girl closed her eyes

and went inside

to the center of herself.

And right away

it seemed that Jesus was there,

looking at her with pride and tenderness.

And he was holding . . .

THREADBEAR.

The grown-up little girl was

astonished. What could this mean?

And then slowly, slowly she understood.

"Jesus, you were there . . . in Threadbear!

You listened and cried with me in the closet.

You were angry at my mother and father

when the bad things happened.

You held my memories

until I was ready for them.

When I was holding onto Threadbear, you were holding onto ME."

And she wept — this time for joy.

Then, deep in the center of herself, she saw the lovely picture of Jesus and the children. Only this time she was in the picture; and Jesus, who was still holding Threadbear, was inviting her to sit on his lap.

Shyly she crept

nearer . . . and nearer . . . **and nearer . . .**

and finally to where he was waiting for her.

Jesus picked her up and held her close.

Both the terrified little girl and the grown-up

woman were there on his lap. All of her was

being loved and spoken to without any words.

It was simply wonderful.

And right then, it seemed that all her life-long

ache for love was finally met.

As she rested there, some of her tension, fear

and shame left her every time she breathed out.

As she breathed in, empty, icy places inside were

filled with marvelous warmth.

When she was finished,

Helper reminded her that she could ask to

sit on Jesus' lap again. Helper said that the

experience of Jesus holding her and

Threadbear formed her very own

sacred picture. Her inner icon of healing,

there for her to gaze at anytime she wished.

And so she learned to pray from the center

of herself. Sometimes there were no words, yet

other times Jesus seemed to speak words she

could hear with her heart:

"It was never your fault."

"You are my beloved child."

"I have always loved you."

In this way she learned to speak to Jesus from her heart.

Chapter X

One day

she spoke inside herself to Jesus,

"I know you love me

and that you were always there.

So why didn't you stop my father?

Why didn't you make my mother

see what was going on?"

Jesus looked at her with great love.

"Remember how I didn't force you to sit on

my lap but waited for you to come closer? "

she felt him say. "In the same way I set your

parents free to choose what they would do

with their lives. I invited your mother and

father to love you tenderly, because that's what

I wanted for you — and for them.

I was sad when they kept saying 'no'."

This answer helped the grown-up little girl

quite a lot. She knew that she would never

fully understand the answer to such an

enormous question. But the more she was able

to let Jesus love her, the less she had to have

complete answers.

For God was healing her heart,

and that was far more important to her.

By this time

she was feeling much, much better.

She had some close friends.

She was finding some ways to have fun.

She was enjoying life more than ever before.

Part of feeling better was that she could no

longer pretend with her parents. She knew,

for example, that if she ever had children

she would never let them be alone with her

father, not even for a minute.

But for now,

she didn't want to see her parents

or even call them. Most of all

she didn't want to hug her father.

So she didn't,

even though he expected it, and asked her

what was the matter.

"Should I tell them?" she wondered.

Helper said it was for her to decide when and

if she wanted to talk to them.

"Should I tell them?

Is it the right time?" she asked Jesus.

And she could feel a YES in her heart.

But even so,

it was a long time before she had the courage

to say anything at all.

It was very scary even to think of talking to

them about it.

But one day

she was feeling very brave.

She told her father:

"I remember what you did to me.

I'm not going to pretend it didn't happen.

It did, and I've been hurt."

She told her mother:

"You hurt me by not seeing what was

going on and not protecting me."

Her father said:

"I don't know what you are talking about."

Her mother said:

"Don't make up stories."

But the grown-up little girl knew that she had spoken the truth

and that it was not her job to get her father and mother to believe her.

Speaking the truth felt clean and powerful.

She told some of her new friends what she had done.

They cheered,

and took her out to dinner to celebrate.

Chapter XI

By now a great deal of healing had taken place. Yet there was more to come.

One day she heard, as if for the first time, words from the Lord's Prayer —

"And forgive us our sins,
as we forgive those
who sin against us."

These words seemed to speak directly to her heart, yet she knew she couldn't do what the words asked of her. She had heard so many sermons on forgiving your enemies, and they just made her feel guilty and wrong. To forgive seemed like saying that what her parents did was perfectly okay. It meant that she would make herself weak again.

Even so,

she had tried and tried to forgive her mother

and father, but every time she even thought of

forgiving, she would just get mad all over

again.

She couldn't do it. They had hurt her too

much. She went to see Helper.

"I can't forgive them," she sobbed.

"I know I'm supposed to, but I just can't do it."

And to her surprise Helper replied,

"Of course you can't."

"The last part of forgiveness, when you let

go of the poison, only happens because the

Holy Spirit gives you the grace to do it. The

first part, letting yourself get rid of your anger

by going all the way to the bottom of it —

you've been working on that for a long time.

Real forgiveness is a process,

and it can't be faked.

Or rushed.

"Finally though,

God will help you forgive deeply

if you ask for it."

She listened, feeling hopeful and hopeless
at the same time.

"I don't even know if I WANT to forgive
them," she cried.

"I can't make myself want to, can I?"

"No," Helper said, "but tell me, what
happens to you when you get angry at them?"

The grown-up little girl thought a minute.

"I feel strong. I know who I am.
I used to be a scared little girl. Now I'm a
strong, angry woman. And I don't want to
go back!"

Helper replied, "Yes, of course. Anger makes
you feel strong. It helps you get well. And that's
good. Maybe it's not yet time to let go of it.
Or maybe God is inviting you to give up your
anger now so even more healing can happen."

The grown-up little girl thought and prayed

about all this for several weeks.

Did she dare to let go of the very thing

that made her feel so good?

Did forgiving mean that all the hurts didn't matter?

That she herself didn't matter?

Would she have to pretend again?

Would she have to hug her father

and smile sweetly at her mother?

And how could she forgive them

if they weren't even SORRY?

She thought deeply and prayed some more.

Surely being whole meant that she wouldn't

have to pretend, she mused.

Instead she would be free to be honest.

It didn't mean she would have to go to their

house if she didn't want to.

Being whole meant knowing that of course

she mattered.

Forgiving just meant letting go of the poison

and allowing God to grow love in her.

Even if they never, ever said they were sorry.

Once again she decided she could trust Jesus. So the next time she saw Helper she said that she was tired of spending so much energy on what had happened in the past. It was indeed time to move on with her life.

So she and Helper asked God to help her forgive. And then Jesus appeared in her heart, as he had so often. This time he had two children with him. She didn't recognize them at first, but then suddenly she realized:

"That's my mother and father
when they were children!"

As she looked at them, she could see that they were scared and crying. Her mother's dress was stained and bloody. Her father's clothes were also a mess, and he moved like he had been hurt.

Suddenly she knew that both of them had been abused as children. No one in the family had ever, *ever* spoken about such a thing. But she knew in her bones it was true.

The grown-up little girl
had the strongest feeling
of wanting to hold and comfort them.

Then in her mind's eye she saw her parents at their present age. They looked old and tired, but underneath the grown-up little girl saw two hurting children. She was surprised she could feel love . . . and compassion for them.

But she burst out, "I don't care if they WERE abused! They should have gotten help as adults. There's no excuse for abusing your child."

And Jesus said, "Yes. There are reasons, but no excuses. What they did was wrong."

These words had a ring of truth and she took some time to let them in.

Then Jesus asked her, "Will you let me do the work of forgiveness in you, so you can be healed?" And taking a deep breath, she said, "Yes, I'm willing. I can't do it myself, but it's okay with me if you do it."

And slowly, slowly, over time

years of poison drained away.

Chapter XII

Many made-up stories end with
". . . and she lived happily ever after."
But real life stories aren't like that. She had to
keep on asking that Jesus do the work of
forgiveness in her, until at last it was finished.
Her fears went away only gradually and it
was quite a while before she felt really safe.

Sometimes, nowadays, the grown-up little
girl experiences anger, sadness, fear, or hurt.
But much more often her life shines with faith
and peace and joy.

Because she is alive, she has much growing
to do. Every day she prays for healing, and to
become more and more like Jesus.

Best of all, she has found out that when
there is deep healing, the Holy Spirit does a
marvelous thing:

Pain is transformed into giftedness.

She has discovered in herself a very special gift of working with hurting children. She listens to them and holds them and prays that they will be healed. Sometimes she tells them the story of Threadbear.

She knows that some hurting children never had a Threadbear of their own. So she helps each of them to discover their special way of how God loved them and helped them to survive.

Some had other grown-ups who loved them.

Some had imaginary playmates.

Some had been able to let parts of themselves remember so that the rest of them could forget. And others found the tiny, tiny place in the very center of themselves where they were never touched by the bad things.

One of her greatest joys is to see children being healed by Jesus.

She feels very blessed to be a Helper.

And what of Threadbear?

Threadbear has a very special place of

honor in her home. She looks at

Threadbear every day to remember how

Jesus cares for her, no matter what.

Sometimes she still sleeps with Threadbear.

Now when they talk, Threadbear tells her

again the story of how wonderfully she has

been healed. And each time she hears it,

she is thankful all over again.

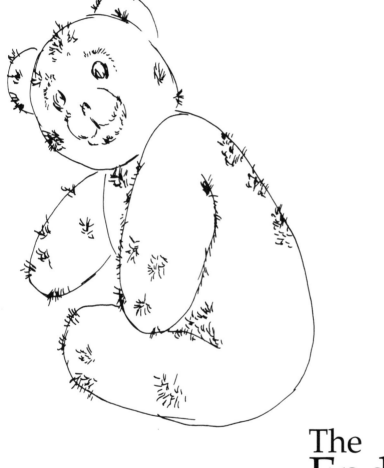

The
End FOR NOW . . .

ABOUT
THE AUTHOR

■

Tilda Norberg, an ordained United Methodist minister, combines Gestalt Psychotherapy with healing prayer and spiritual direction. Teaching, writing, leading retreats and workshops, and her private practice form and shape her ministry. She has had over 25 years of experience working with survivors of sexual abuse. She is the author with Dr. Robert Webber of *Stretch Out Your Hand: Exploring Healing Prayer*, published by United Church Press, 1990, and soon to be reprinted by Upper Room Press.

ABOUT
THE ARTIST

■

Joyce Thomas is an independent illustrator and designer living in New York City. In addition to her artwork, she leads art workshops and retreats to free innate creativity and uncover new and exciting ways of experiencing God. Joyce is currently writing and illustrating a new book on the lighter side of prayer.

For More Information on:

■

Gestalt Pastoral Care workshops and training
please call or write:

Tilda Norberg
(718) 273-4941
78 Clinton Avenue
Staten Island, NY 10301

■

Artwork, Arts and Spirituality workshops and retreats
please call or write:

Joyce Thomas
(212) 472-0379
353 East 83rd Street - #11E
New York, NY 10028

Made in the USA
San Bernardino, CA
30 June 2015

ABSOLUTELY AMA**Z**ING eBOOKS

AbsolutelyAmazingEbooks.com
or AA-eBooks.com

ABOUT THE AUTHOR

R.K. Simpson lives in Alexandria, Virginia, with his wife Patty. He is a graduate of Dartmouth College and a veteran of the Marine Corps and the war in Vietnam. He served as a diplomat in several of our embassies in Europe and Africa for over twenty years. Upon retiring from the government, he worked as a pediatric nurse for fifteen years. He has three adult children.

WEBLEY .45

AND OTHER SHORT STORIES

R.K. Simpson

ABSOLUTELY AMA⚡ING eBOOKS

ABSOLUTELY AMAZING eBOOKS

Published by Whiz Bang LLC, 926 Truman Avenue, Key West, Florida 33040, USA.

For information contact:
Publisher@AbsolutelyAmazingEbooks.com

ISBN-13: 978-1503115101
ISBN-10: 1503115100

To Patricia with love and gratitude

TABLE OF CONTENTS

WEBLEY .45

AND OTHER SHORT STORIES

WEBLEY .45

Grandpa Pat heard their chatter that fateful morning and glanced up from his book. He watched them through the screen door walking in the sunshine across his front lawn. Faded cut-off shorts, worn sneakers, tan arms, and deep conversation. They marched in lockstep up the front steps and across the porch. Two souls in sync, he thought.

Ellie, who was eleven, had azure eyes, full of mischief and appeal. Pat called her 'Squirt' because she fizzed with energy and ideas. "I know what we can do," she had suggested earlier that morning. "Let's catch some lightning bugs, let 'em loose in the movie theater, and watch 'em fly to the projector light." Pat's grandson Max was one year younger than Ellie and always amused by her imagination, but he was a full partner in their relationship. He read all the time and could keep Ellie's attention by telling her things like how caterpillars become butterflies and by showing her how the Japanese fold paper into dainty, bird-like figures. Their friendship felt right; it had balance.

Grandfather Pat liked to muse occasionally over his relationship with his grandson. There was a delicate symmetry to it, he thought, life's beginning and end, beneficial to both but fragile and fleeting. Each found his role in their relationship almost effortless. As an infant, Max had bonded with his grandfather instantly. When Pat was with him, Max was happy. It was as simple as that and

everyone noticed it. Pat had fallen for the child too but, burdened by his past, he had been wary at first. He had grown up an orphan and had been unnerved by fatherhood when his own child was born. Looking back, he felt he never really got the hang of it. Then grandfatherhood had barged into his life and reminded him again of his inadequacies as a parent. It also offered him a chance at redemption, however, and knowing how infrequently second chances come along, Pat had jumped at the opportunity. He offered his unwed daughter his services as her son's daycare provider, realizing he was actually volunteering to be the boy's *de facto* father.

This commitment rejuvenated him. As his doubts began to fade, his heart began to melt. Everything about the boy touched him: the infant's tiny, insistent grip on his finger; his miraculous eight-pound body nestled in his arms, sharing its warmth; and his grandson's miniature features forming expressions similar to those on the grizzled face looking down at him. Studying the infant one evening, Pat realized the little boy brought out in him a kind of love he had never known as a child, and he vowed then and there to do everything he could to spare Max the kind of loneliness he had known in his youth.

He threw himself into his new role. When Max was barely old enough to talk, he began to tell him fanciful bedtime stories. He conjured up Black Bart, a philanthropist-bank robber with a monkey accomplice, and Alice, a boy with a girl's name who invented a paint that made him invisible. The stories were full of adventure and ethical dilemmas. Max would listen so hard he could hardly fall asleep afterward. In the afternoons, Pat would

read him the classics, using funny accents to turn himself into Uncle Remus and Br'er Rabbit and the other critters. He gave Oliver Twist a squeaky voice with an English accent that made Max giggle, and he peppered Long John Silver's speech with real swear words. Before long, Max could mimic the characters too and swear like a pirate.

They also worked together year-round in Pat's garage. Max loved the place with its pungent smells of moist earth, oil, and paint; its drawers and boxes full of nuts and bolts and useful junk from previous projects; its vast peg board where Grandpa hung his tools, each in its precise place; and its scarred workbench where Max – standing on a chair – helped his Grandpa work on his row boat and learned to tie knots. On the first day of kindergarten, he said to the teacher without preamble, "My Grandpa taught me to tie my shoes. Wanna see?"

~~~

"Hey, you turkeys," Pat said as Ellie and Max pushed through the screen door that sunny morning. "How about a blueberry muffin?"

"Yeah, cool," they said in unison.

"Can we play in the attic?" Ellie asked.

"Sure, go on up," Pat replied. "We'll make some lunch later."

Ellie and Max loved to play in Pat's old house. To them its scents of decline and the passage of time whispered of mystery and ancient history. They could get lost among the musty books and covered furniture in unlit rooms. They could be transported by yellowing photos of Pat with his football mates, stern and determined in their leather

helmets, or with his army buddies, jaunty and down on a knee in front of their tank.

Most of all they loved the attic. They ascended to it on creaky stairs. It was flooded with a ghoulish light filtered through two Plexiglas skylights that had turned yellowish-purple from long exposure to the sun. It had a slanted ceiling and a woody smell. The roof made eerie noises when sticks blew across it and when the television antenna wires tugged at their metal moorings.

"Man, this place is weird" Ellie said with a sneaky smile. The unearthly light had turned her tan skin the color of a bruise.

"We can use this for the rocket ship," Max said moving to his right and edging along a footed bathtub. "But we gotta find more stuff." Ellie moved to her left, scanning the area in search of rocket material.

"This big box will be good," he said. "We can put it on top of the bathtub and use it as a reentry capsule."

Ellie was listening, but she had begun to investigate a footlocker. Its latch was locked, but a key hung from a ring of flexible wire twisted around a rotting leather handle. She untwisted the wire, pushed the key into the lock, and turned it. She loved moments of uncertainty like this when she had some control but not enough to guarantee the outcome. She stood as she lifted the lid of the old chest and peered inside. Wedged beside a pile of folded shirts was a blue-black pistol. She reached for it instinctively and was conscious of its heft as she turned toward Max and raised it, straightening her arms as she had seen policemen do on television.

Within the confines of the attic, the report had a force of its own. In that first nano-second, when the minutest differences in their positions might have changed the outcome, when Ellie's fingers were beginning their reflexive release of the weapon, a wall of sound hit her and she began to fall. The .45 caliber slug ripped an inch from the artery in Max's groin, shattered his sacral spine, lifted him off his feet, and spun him counterclockwise onto a blue bicycle. He felt no pain. He was distantly aware that his arm was tangled in the spokes of a wheel. He tried to push himself off the bike, but he felt no resistance from the floor. He was floating, looking through reddish brown lenses.

~~~

Even before the funeral service – which most of the town attended – Pat began to decline. Merciless memories ricocheted in his brain: the pad of sneakers crossing the porch, then climbing the attic stairs; the hum and sibilance of their youthful voices; his own voice ringing out day and night, "Sure, go ahead up"; and, the muffled sound of the shot. Although Pat had not thought of that gun in years, the instant he heard the shot, he knew what had happened. Since then, grief and guilt had been working to destroy him.

But his wife Sue, infirm though she was, fought back. She abandoned her bed to lie next to her husband at night to hold him so he would not will himself to die. She urged him to be strong, even though he had no appetite, no energy, and sleep defied him, despite the pills. Those football-shaped tranquilizers could knock him off his feet, but they could not turn off the pictures or turn down the

noise. When Sue urged him to talk to her about these things, shame moved in and silenced him.

"You know I really need you to live," she said to him in desperation one afternoon. "This isn't only about you!" Pat focused on her face. It was more familiar to him than his own face, yet never in their forty-some years had he seen the shadow of fear play across its kind features. He loved her and wanted to still those fears, but he could not find words for her.

"You didn't kill him, Hon," she said after a long pause. She leaned forward and put her hand on his knee to soften the harshness of the verb.

"I made it possible though."

"What do you mean?" she asked, withdrawing her hand as her back stiffened.

"I stole that gun. Then I brought it home, hid it – loaded, for God's sake – and forgot all about it!"

Sue leaned forward and put her hand on his knee again. They looked at each other in the ringing silence. She would remember the boniness of his thigh, the sagging bookshelf behind him, the sun's rays angling in through the blinds from low on the horizon throwing bars of light and shadow across his thin frame. "It can't be that simple," she said. "Talk to me."

Pat sighed deeply – shuddered really – as he thought back over the years and began to tell a story Sue had never heard. His first memories, he said, were of the Catholic orphanage. He arrived as an infant, too young even to remember who brought him or why. Apparently, he was all alone in the world, as he did not receive a single visitor or letter during his ten years there.

Life was hard in the orphanage. It offered little comfort or kindness, but it did teach Pat he could endure difficult circumstances. He endured rheumatic fever one spring, even as it took the lives of several of his classmates. In addition, he endured those frigid, desperately depressing winters. To lift his spirits and alleviate the cold he would sneak away from his chores whenever possible and visit the barn. There he would savor the animals' warmth and their kind faces, and he would stand barefoot in fresh cow droppings to warm his feet. He endured by his wits, will, and gained confidence that would help him through the difficult times to come.

Then one morning, just after his tenth birthday, a man arrived at the orphanage with legal papers and instead of eating his oatmeal, as usual, Pat found himself bouncing along in a pickup truck, his eyes watering from gas fumes and cigarette smoke. "You can call me Uncle John," the driver said without looking at Pat. "Your Pa was my sister's husband. I'm takin' you home to live with us." Uncle John was as hard and expressionless as a cue ball, and he saw the world in black and white only, as Pat was about to learn.

When Pat halted momentarily, Sue placed a hand on his, leaned forward, and stood incrementally, wincing slightly from the back pain. Pat arose quickly to help her, but she declined. The sun had dipped below the horizon leaving the room dimly lit and chilly. She shuffled to a wall switch and flipped on the lights. As she turned, Pat caught her eye and a look that meant 'give me a moment.' When she had eased herself back into her comfortable chair, Pat continued.

"The first day in my new home I worked in Uncle John's garage, as I did every Saturday," he said. He was not the only new employee that day. Uncle John had just hired a man to pump gas. He was a lanky fellow with sad, sunken eyes and stooped shoulders. Long hairs on the back of his neck poked through his frayed collar. Early in the afternoon, Pat noticed the man drift over to his car with a wrench in his hand and return without it.

"Where you going with my wrench?" Uncle John asked.

"Just wanna borrow it t' fix something at home," the man said. Uncle John swung so fast Pat could not recall seeing him move at all. The man dropped straight to his knees, his eyes open but vacant, then pitched forward like a rag doll. Uncle John stared down at the limp body until it moved, then shouted at it to get out. Pat never forgot the brutality of that act and he took it as a warning.

John's wife, Darlene, feared him too and treated him with humiliating deference. Pat's arrival was just another potential hazard to her. She had to be careful not to ignite one of her husband's jealous rages by being too affectionate with Pat. So she only hinted at her feelings for him by calling him 'Sonny' and by treating him kindly. She washed his clothes, prepared his meals, and when John was not at home she spoke to him of his father. Pat loved these conversations and did all he could to strengthen their relationship, but ultimately fear always intervened and had its way.

One fall evening when Pat was almost seventeen, he found Darlene sprawled on the kitchen floor when he entered the back door after football practice. She lay there

pale and disoriented, her skirts flung high on one thigh. Pat looked at her with concern, but hesitated to go to her because she did not ask for help and he had never touched her. At that moment, they heard Uncle John's pickup crunch along the gravel driveway.

"God, get me off the floor," she said, more a plea to God Himself than to Pat. He bent down quickly and helped her up. By the time Uncle John walked in, she was on her feet again peeling potatoes. Pat was seated at the kitchen table and though the scene was unremarkable, Uncle John sensed tension.

"What's wrong here?" he asked. The question hung in the silence like a guilty verdict. Pat shrugged. Darlene tightened her grip on the edge of the sink.

"Answer me! You still moaning about last night?" This time the threatening words were directed at Darlene.

"She isn't feeling good," Pat said.

"Git to your chores in the barn," Uncle John said in a chilling monotone while moving toward Pat. In reliving this incident, Pat remembered Uncle John moving toward him like a cat, loose and fluid, without a sound, his eyes, devoid of expression, locked on Pat's.

"But I..."

The punch traveled too far. It was averted by the quickness of youth and the total focus fear can bring. It threw Uncle John off balance, but only for an instant. His next punch slammed into Pat's ribs and drove him through the kitchen doorway into the living room. He was still standing but he found it almost impossible to draw breath.

"Git to the barn."

Pat grabbed an iron fire stoker from the hearth and held it in two hands as one would hold a shovel. He pointed the sharp end at John's chest and stepped forward. A spell settled over him; he became aware of Uncle John's breathing, his stance, his smell, even his dilated pupils. He was unafraid. If John charged him, he would kill him. He knew it. He would drive that stoker clean through his chest just to the left of center. He focused his full attention on that point on John's chest, tightened his grip, and instinctively took another step forward, giving John less time and space to fend off the stoker.

"Look," John said, extending his hands forward palms down, "I wanna talk to Darlene...*alone.*" Expression returned to his voice and his eyes. "I'm not gonna hurt her, don't worry. Now make yourself scarce."

It was a truce, something Uncle John had never suggested, at least in Pat's presence. Pat sensed he would not be struck again, but he kept the stoker pointed at John's heart and continued to face him until John turned away.

All was quiet that night, but Pat did not sleep. He lay awake deciding whether to leave or stay. He disliked the idea of running away – it seemed cowardly – and he knew he should finish his senior year. But, he knew also he had come perilously close to killing a man that afternoon, and the next time the outcome might be different. This fact trumped every reason he could imagine for staying. And so he convinced himself to leave. His only regret was Darlene. He felt guilty for abandoning her. During their years together, they had forged an unspoken, us-against-him

alliance, which had helped keep them from harm. That night as Pat lay in bed considering their pact, he thought of a mantra he hoped would keep conflict at bay as he set off alone into the world: *Be Ready For Trouble*.

"That was Uncle John's legacy to me," Pat said.

"Pretty pathetic," Sue replied. Although references to his childhood always bothered her, Sue was delighted he was talking. It was the most he had said in weeks.

~~~

The next day Pat slipped his ancestral ties and left Uncle John's world. At 3 a.m., he crept out of the house with only a small suitcase and his newly minted mantra. He made his way to the county road behind John's house and began walking. When the first headlights appeared over a rise, he stuck out his thumb, and a newspaper deliveryman braked to a stop in front of him. 'Ah, a piece of good luck to start my travels,' Pat thought as he climbed aboard. Later that morning 200 miles from home he lied about his age to an Army recruiter and found himself boarding a Greyhound for boot camp.

Pat did not find basic training difficult. The sergeants who yelled at him were pussycats compared to Uncle John. He knew their words and actions were fired for effect, not for real. At seventeen, he was strong and fit. He enjoyed their weekly 'forced marches' and flew over the obstacle course fastest in his platoon. Back home, where everybody had a rifle, he was a natural. He could drop a dove on the wing with buckshot four out of five times and he could hit a squirrel with a .22 almost as often. So, the stationary four-inch bullseyes on the rifle range targets presented no challenge. In recognition of his high standing in basic

training the Army promoted him to private first class, gave him two weeks leave, and orders to Fort Knox.

During the war, hitchhikers in uniform were almost guaranteed rides. So, having little money and nowhere to spend his two weeks, Pat marched off the parade field immediately after graduation ceremonies, duffel bag on his shoulder, and stuck out a thumb for Kentucky. By late afternoon, he had covered more than one hundred miles with three rides. Ride number four, a sedate Buick sedan, pulled onto the gravelly shoulder as the cold January sun sank behind the Allegheny Mountains. Pat slid in.

"Thanks for the ride, sir. Much obliged."

"Where are you headed, soldier?" The question posed elegantly in its British accent. The driver, pudgy and pale, gripped the wheel delicately. His keyhole mouth pursed and his eyebrows arched as he glanced sidelong at his passenger.

"Fort Knox, Kentucky."

"Ah, Fort Knox," he said, allowing his eyebrows to settle again below the upper horn rim of his glasses. "If you like I can take you as far as Harlan. Ever heard of it?"

"Yes. I remember reading about it in history class this year and seeing some pretty gruesome pictures of it in Life magazine. Are you from there?"

"No," said the driver of the Buick, "but as a law professor, I know something about it." Harlan was Appalachia, he explained, a coal mining county, and the scene of violent labor unrest. At the turn of the century, big corporations had begun exploiting the mountaineers for the timber on their land and the minerals beneath it. They 'negotiated' the rights to oil, slate, iron, and gas on

private land in exchange for new appliances, home improvements or, at best, a new truck. Logging companies felled ancient tulip poplar, red oak, hickory, hard maple, cedar, pine and chestnut for a pittance a tree. Explosions, falling rock and faulty machinery injured and killed workers and scarred the land. In a culture where families remember insults for generations and men pull knives when someone kicks their dog, it was not long before blood began to spill.

By the time Pat slid out of the warm sedan shortly before sunrise the next morning, the professor had finished his history lecture and run out of tales of shootouts, arson, and murder in Harlan county. It was exciting entertainment, but the anti-government attitude of the local folks made Pat feel conspicuous in his uniform as he hauled his duffle out of the back seat.

"Thanks for the ride," he said.

"Thanks for the company, lad. Be careful around here."

Sue roused herself again from her chair. "Hang on, Hon," she said, "I got to take a pill. You want a cup of tea? A blanket? Anything?"

Pat shook his head. "No, thanks," he said, knowing his answer was pointless. She returned in five minutes, covered his lap with a plaid blanket, and handed him a cup of hot tea. Pat smiled and sipped.

"I remember watching that Buick disappear behind a Beechnut Chewing Tobacco billboard," he said pensively, "and feeling kind of lonely." A chill wind swept litter along the curb and a dog barked in the distance. Pat's eyes felt gritty and his neck and shoulders ached from hauling his

duffel bag. There were no pedestrians on the streets yet, but a couple of pickups passed and turned at the next corner. Pat heaved his duffel onto his better shoulder and followed them.

Setter's Café was a plain brick building with a handwritten sign painted on its window, *Eats Are Better At Setter's*. The room was warm, the atmosphere sweet with aromas of coffee, bacon, and biscuit. He moved across the creaky floor, around a big Franklin stove, and perched on a stool at the end of a long counter. He spun halfway around to observe his surroundings. Plain tables, mostly empty still; a few customers, all men, all plain, skinny, white men with serious eyes, stubble, raw hands, worn overalls and flannel shirts, sitting in groups, drinking coffee black, smoking their cigarettes to nubbins, exchanging somber thoughts quietly now and then.

"What'll you have?" Pat turned to face a plain woman in a gray dress and rimless glasses.

"I'd like some breakfast, please, ma'am. I'm real hungry ... eggs, grits, bacon, biscuit, whatever you have'll be good." She gave an almost imperceptible nod and turned away. She returned with a heavy cup of black coffee. "Reckon you want one of these too," she said and turned away before he could say thanks.

The food came soon and more men drifted in, but the sound of conversation did not increase much. A nod was the standard greeting. The waitress brought food to those few who wanted it without being asked or acknowledged. She knew all the men and what they ate; they knew she did not want to gab. Pat ate in silence too, following Setter's breakfast etiquette, and began to feel better. As he poured

honey from a quart jar onto his second warm biscuit, he became aware of a presence next to him.

"What 'er you doin'?" The question did not sound friendly. Pat turned toward the man, a shot of adrenaline heightening his senses, but the man seemed to be looking beyond him. "Yeah, I'm a-lookin' at *you*," he said, noting Pat's hesitance and turned to face him. He was walleyed. One eye looked intently at Pat; the other aimed blindly off to the right. "Like I say, I got one eye a-lookin' at cha and anotherin' a-looking fer ya." The man said it without a trace of humor. "You spoon that thar honey outa that thar jar," he instructed. "You go a-pourin' it and it'll never stop a-runnin' down the side – have yoursef one unholy mess." He sipped his coffee and continued to look at Pat and beyond. "Whar you headin'?"

"I'm hitching to Fort Knox, sir."

The man did not reply. He turned back to the counter, put both elbows up, and sipped. Pat glanced toward him once and saw his jaw muscle twitch. He spooned some honey as directed and enjoyed his biscuit. He asked for another coffee and thought how far into the past his previous life had faded.

"You'll be a-goin' through London then, London, Kentucky, that is," the man said. "Ah ain't a-goin' that fer, but ah'm a-goin' that direction cuz ah gotta do me some bidness up to Salt Gum and Wullum. Ah kin carry you in that direction if'n you want." As he spoke, the man stood, but not exactly upright. He seemed to be partially twisted above the waist so as he rose he turned and tilted slightly away from Pat. "You comin'?"

15

"Yeah, I'm comin'," Pat heard himself mimic. He had no reason not to accept the offer except Uncle John's influence whispering, 'Be ready for trouble'. Pat appraised the man as he followed him out the door to the truck, telling himself that in case of trouble he had size and youth on the man to say nothing of two good eyes and a straight back. But he was not fully reassured. He noticed also the lightness of the man's step. Despite his flaws and a winter coat, the man moved gracefully and efficiently, a bantamweight in heavy robes.

The pickup had no rear license plate and the running board gave slightly under Pat's weight as he climbed onto the front seat. The old Chevy had known some characters and seen some action. It had weathered to a blend of soft, nondescript grays, and it pitched nose-down, a deformity probably caused by bad shocks, Pat thought. But it cranked up willingly and rumbled away from town like an old gray mare heading for her barn. Only after he swung off the macadam road onto a two-lane dirt surface did the man appear to relax.

"You got kin in these parts?" he asked.

"No, sir. I've never been in Kentucky before."

"Don't know nobody here then?"

"No, sir. Not a soul."

"You in the Army, eh?"

"Yes, sir. In the Army now."

"You ain't a-workin' fer the federal gubmint, are you?"

"Yep. That's right," Pat said.

"And you shore you ain't got no kin round here?"

"Not so far as I know. How 'bout you, sir? You got lots of family in the area?"

"Yeah. Born and bred in this county."

"Nice country," Pat said. The narrow road rose and fell and wove its way through the valley, a narrow ribbon of brown in a study of grays. The only evidence of modern life were the ranks of tarred pine telephone poles, which sprouted from one side of the road or the other depending on the steepness of the embankments.

"Ah reckon, but we got more trouble than a sack a snakes nowadays. Damn Feds and them rich Yankees come down har sweet talkin' us and a-lyin' smoother'n spit on a brass doorknob. You cain't trust not a damn one of 'em. If'n they don't stay up north and mind thar own bidness, trouble'll be swallowin' more of 'em up sure as Death."

Despite the molasses-thick twang, Pat had no trouble feeling the heat of the man's words. He did not reply, and the man's death reference hung in silence for several miles.

"Ah'm stoppin' up har a piece to do me a chore. You kin jist make yoursef to home in the truck."

After several more miles of lulling curves and dips and rises in the road, the man pulled into a clearing, alit from the cab as softly as a bird, and disappeared through an opening in a giant rhododendron bush.

Pat looked beyond it and saw a low A-frame building, its wood seasoned so naturally it seemed part of the sprawling sycamores and dense brush surrounding it. He could make out a window just below the roof peak and a barn door below it. The heat of the animals below would help warm the humans above on days like this. Pat settled

in to wait. Nearly thirty hours had passed since he had rolled out of bed that last day at boot camp.

Funny, he thought half-conscious, there's no noise in there. No people.

He awoke with a start, unaware for an instant of where he was. He listened and heard only the rustle of dead leaves and the winter wind in the branches. There was no sign or sound of the man.

Shit, thought Pat, how did I end up way out here?

Suddenly the man's gaunt face appeared in the passenger side window. He had approached his old truck noiselessly from the rear.

"C'mear," he beckoned, and headed into the rhododendron. Pat opened the door and put a leg out, but hesitated. The man seemed to sense his caution.

"C'mear. Ah need some hep."

Pat followed him along a path he had been unable to see from the truck and into the barn. It was dark inside, the air moist and pungent. The smells carried Pat back to the barn at the orphanage and to the fear he felt when the Rector caught him there.

"Wait a jiff," the man said, and scurried up a ladder onto the floor above.

Pat stood still, listening to the footsteps above him until a length of chain dropped through the opening in the ceiling like a huge dead snake and coiled with a metallic splat near the foot of the ladder. The man followed, scampering down agile as a monkey.

"This har chain's too heavy and awkerd fer me to carry to the truck alone. Figured t'gether we could carry it out thar on the pallet."

"Sure," Pat said, vaguely relieved by the innocence of the chore. "Whatcha going to use the chain for?"

"Oh, good Lordy, boy. Plenty of uses for good chain," the man said as they hauled it down the path. They deposited it and the pallet in the truck bed next to Pat's duffel and climbed back into the cab.

"How 'bout a chaw," the man asked pulling the packet of Redman from his hip pocket.

What the hell, Pat thought. He had seen men chew tobacco at the garage back home so he knew how to look like a chewer, how to peel back the silver paper, bite off a plug and pull it away with a sideways tug. He bit off a big piece, figuring you just chew a few times to soften it, then tongue it down into the pocket between his teeth and cheek. But he was not ready for the rancid fluids that squirted up into his sinuses and ran out his nose with that first chew. He gagged almost from his toes; tears welled up and spilled down his cheeks; he gasped for breath. In a panic he cranked down the window while clearing his throat to spit, but he did not crank fast enough and spit against the inside of the window. Finally he thrust his head out and over the side and spit again. The man stifled a chuckle.

"Jesus, Mary, and Joseph," he said.

Pat tongued his chaw down hard into his cheek and squeezed his eyes shut.

"Just went down the wrong tube," he said wiping the tears away, but he did not spit out the chaw.

Sue giggled at the image of her young Pat trying to chew tobacco with a hillbilly, but to her dismay she felt tears beginning to roll down her cheeks too. She wrapped

a hand over her mouth and turned away from Pat, trying to hide her emotions. There was something in her gesture during that brief moment that hurt Pat's feelings and made him realize the degree to which he had kept her from his thoughts and feelings since Max's death. He felt ashamed and his own emotions welled up.

After several seconds and a deep breath he managed to say, "Sorry, Hon ..." but no more.

"That's okay," she said. "I understand."

They sat in silence for a moment until Pat was ready. "The man was still shaking his head in disbelief," Pat began, "as he pulled out of the clearing and shifted through the gears." The tobacco in Pat's cheek and the blasts of cold air he felt when they rolled down their windows to spit kept Pat awake. Snow flurries swirled intermittently. By late morning he realized the telephone wires that had floated above them in long, graceful scallops were gone from the gray sky.

God, we're beyond reach now, Pat thought, and for the first time felt a twinge of fear. *Be Ready For Trouble*: the mantra hovered like a vulture. He had little idea where he was. No one else did either, he realized, except the crippled mountain man next to him.

They crossed a narrow river and a couple of creeks on rickety wooden bridges. They rolled by an inlet where five or six charred car carcasses lay on their sides half submerged, windows smashed.

"Federales' cars," the man said as he slowed to a crawl and gestured with his head so Pat would not miss them.

They rumbled by small houses, some with washing machines and divans on front porches, passed signs

painted on teetering sheds that said 'Jesus Is Coming' and 'Beechnut: Chews Best, Tastes Best.' Finally, they turned off the dirt road onto an overgrown trail. Branches clawed at the old gray pickup as it plowed forward. They stopped in front of a low cinderblock building in relatively good repair.

"You wait here, Chaw. Don't go nowhar," the man ordered using the nickname for the first time. Pat rolled down his window and listened – only the sounds of the breeze in bare branches again and a river rushing in the distance. Then he heard men's voices, conversation but unintelligible over the sounds of the holler. Pat opened the door, but stopped with one leg on the running board. He hesitated to disobey the man's instruction. He looked around the cab and saw the keys dangling in the ignition. I could just drive out of here, he thought. Drive to a main road, leave the truck, and hitch another ride. Might be safest. Then he saw them, two men rounding the corner of the building and approaching the truck with its owner.

Pat slid back in and closed the door. One of the men waddled toward him. He was very heavy mostly from the waist down. His fluorscent pinkish face was too small for the puffy body under it and glowed from behind thick glasses. His ball cap had an extra-long visor frayed and bent v-shaped in the middle. It sat too low on his little head. Long white-blond strands of hair hung limply down his neck. The other man was slim and swarthy. His dark eyes were wide-set and hooded. His black hair was slicked down shiny. He smelled strongly of cologne and whiskey and wore clean overalls with a white shirt buttoned at the neck. His brown suit coat pulled shapelessly from his

shoulders under the weight of a pistol in one side pocket, a bottle in the other. The three men gathered at the passenger side door and looked at Pat.

"This here's two a mah friends," the pickup owner said.

"What's your name?" the man with the pistol asked.

"Moynahan," Pat said.

"Ain't heard a no Moynahans in these parts."

"Well, there probably aren't any. I'm not from around here, and like I told him," Pat nodded toward the owner of the truck, "I don't have any kin who live around here." Immediately he thought it might have been a mistake to mention that again.

"That so, sure enough," the man said in a flat tone so Pat could not tell if he were doubting him or expressing relief or maybe pleasure.

"You wanna use the toilet, take a bath, or somethin'?" the pale man asked unexpectedly. Pat stared at the apparition for too long. He knew it, but he could not help it. He was mesmerized by the magnified pink eyes and the triangular bulk. He thought, the last thing I'm going to do is take my clothes off out here in the woods with these three.

"No, thanks. I'm fine. I have a friend in London who's expecting me tonight," he improvised. "I can wash up at his house."

"Suit yoursef, but you git outta that thar' truck now anyhow," the man with the pistol said in his flat tone. Pat felt the prickly sensation begin high on his scalp and slide down his neck like a wave of cold needles. He felt the sweat break under his hair. He knew his hand, cold and

shaky, had pulled the door handle open and that he was standing by the truck, but his balance was uncertain. He bent from the waist and remained for a moment with his hands on his knees.

Pat heard the slim man move toward him, saw his black dress shoes planted directly in front of him, and felt the man's hands grab him and lift him by the shoulders.

"What's a matter, boy, that tobaccy makin' you sick?" the man said, looking him straight in the eye. He pulled the pistol from his pocket and handed it to the owner of the truck. He pulled the bottle from his other pocket, handed it to the albino, and removed his suit coat.

"Take off that thar uniform jacket," the man said, and another wave of needles hit Pat. His heart pounded harder and his dry mouth could not swallow away the painful knot in his throat, but he managed to remove the blouse.

"Give this boy your hanky, Oren," he said as he pulled on the thigh-length khaki jacket. "He's sweatin' like a mule in July. You okay, boy? You want some water? Gib him some water, Oren."

Pat shook his head and leaned against the truck. The man tugged the blouse down, adjusted his shoulders, and strutted around like a field marshal.

"Guess this is 'bout as close as ah'm gonna come to wearin' the uniform. Fits me right good though, don't you reckon, boys?"

"Don't look so good with them overalls, Howard. You look like you was half possum, half coon." Oren grinned with brown teeth, slapped his leg, and fired the pistol up into the black branches for emphasis. The man snatched

his pistol from Oren, nodded and returned the blouse to Pat.

"Boy, you look like you seen a ghost. You're paler 'n ole Matthew here," he said gesturing toward the albino. "You spit out that tobaccy." He reached an empty hand toward the albino who handed him the bottle. "Ah mona keep you alive for while. You take a little drink a' this." Pat tipped the bottle back obediently, sipped and swallowed and felt the fiery fluid burn through the knot in his throat. It warmed his stomach and his face at the same time.

"Thanks," he said searching the man's eyes for his intentions.

"Ah gotta be goin,'" Oren said. "Git in, Chaw. Ah'll see you tonight, right?" The two men nodded and waved as Oren reversed and forwarded his truck several times on the narrow trail until he had it pointing back toward the road.

The old gray truck had no heater. Some warm air from the motor found its way into the cab with the gas fumes, but not much. Pat began to shiver. "You okay, Chaw?" Oren asked. "You gonna be sick?"

"Maybe," Pat said as the effects of the adrenaline, tobacco juice, moonshine and fatigue washed over him. Oren pulled to a stop. Pat stumbled out and leaned his head against the cold metal of the rear fender. He waited, staring down at the dirt and his shoes. The wave of nausea subsided, but he felt light-headed. He stood up straight and took some deep breaths of winter air like his football coach had told him to do before a game. He sat on the running board for a minute with his head between his

knees, and stood again. "Okay," he said through the open door. "Sorry."

He climbed in, slammed the door, and Oren pulled back onto the road. As the miles and minutes fell away, Pat felt fatigue pour over him like warm honey. His eyelids hung heavy as velvet curtains and his head bounced and bobbed off his chest. But he had to stay awake. Slick had said, "I'm going to keep you alive for a while." What did that mean? He repeated his mantra: *Be Ready For Trouble.*

"Uncle John, rearing his ugly head again," Sue interjected. "He's not looking so bad now, is he?"

"Just wait. How are you doing?" Pat asked.

"Fine," she said. "You?"

"Better."

Pat recalled a lonely road that played out before them like an endless string floating, curling, sweeping past ugly mining scars in the valley's sides, past rockslides and gnarled black trees that once bore fruit, past crooked creeks frothing and frigid, racing downstream. Occasionally they would come upon a solitary figure walking on the side of the road hunched against the damp and Oren would slow his truck and lift the index finger from his hand resting atop the steering wheel. He was home. In mid-afternoon, they slowed almost to a stop for a gaggle of school kids of all ages ambling home in the middle of the road.

"This here's Blue Hole," Pat heard Oren say as they glided by a stand of sooty, wood frame houses and a gristmill pumping noise out onto the street. A ghostly figure covered in white mill dust waved at Oren as he

passed and stared at the stranger in uniform on the seat. Less than a mile outside Blue Hole, Oren pulled off the road and into a yard, launching a bevy of chickens into random flight. Feathers and a cacophony of squawks fell from the sky, small faces appeared at the door of a hen house. Pat bolted into full consciousness.

"Ah mona go inside here fer a spell. You kin sleep here if you want, or come on in, either way," Oren said sliding out of the truck.

"I'll just wait here, take a little nap."

He scrutinized Oren's peculiar gait as he crossed the yard scattering chickens again. He walked in a straight line, but his shoulders were not perpendicular to the direction in which he moved. They were several degrees off course, and one shoulder hung well below the other. Half-dreaming, Pat remembered long ago watching a big dog trotting with similar misdirection up the long driveway to the orphanage. Brother Samuel had hustled Pat inside saying the dog was rabid.

"How do you know,? Pat had asked.

"Because he's walking sideways," Brother Samuel had answered. "His brain is sick and can't make his feet walk right."

He had heard the shot shortly thereafter when someone killed the dog.

He slumped too comfortably against the seat and felt himself slip. He was dropping his guard inch by inch, then he lost touch. He slept; he had no idea for how long, but when he awoke, three youthful faces were staring at him through the driver's side window. An adult with a pitchfork stood toward the front of the truck and watched

him through the windshield. Eight cautious, curious eyes watched him wordlessly. Pat looked back, then opened his door and stepped out.

"Hi," he said.

The adult nodded, but the teenagers did not react. They stood fast, staring him down, scowling like kids on a playground before a fight.

"You with the gubmint?" the adult asked as he moved around toward Pat.

"No, sir, not exactly. I'm in the Army. I mean the Army's the government I guess, but... not exactly."

"You ain't with no company, ain't lookin' to buy nothing?"

"No, sir. I don't have money to buy anything."

The man stood motionless studying Pat for a minute or two.

"We ain't lookin' for no trouble," the man said finally, "less'n someone comes a-meddlin'." He let the threat hang, then nodded again and headed off to the house with the youngsters and the pitchfork.

Pat slid back into the truck. I gotta find some way to protect myself out here, he thought. These people are dangerous. They really don't like me being here and they could do away with me way out here and nobody would ever know it.

He looked around the cab with no idea of what he was looking for. The keys were gone. He jumped out and scanned the junk in the truck bed. The chain, some copper tubing, rags, crockery, a dirty pair of overalls, but nothing he could conceivably use as a weapon, not even a screwdriver or a hammer. He sat back in the cab and

rummaged through the glove compartment. A lace handkerchief and a corn cob both covered with dust, a yellowing newspaper article entitled "Battle of Evarts" about a shootout accompanied by a picture of three dead deputy sheriffs lying in ungainly postures near a car.

He leaned forward, head near his knees, and ran a hand blindly under his seat. His fingers hit cold metal. He knew instantly what he had touched. He lifted his head slightly and peered out through the bottom of the windshield at the house. An old woman was now sitting in a rocking chair on the porch. No one else was in sight. He was aware of his short, shallow breathing. His fingers wrapped around the barrel and he pulled it forward from under the seat.

"Holy Moses," he whispered. The revolver lay heavy in his hand. He studied it closely while monitoring the outside for movement and sound: it was a blue-black pistol, .45 caliber, black crosshatched grip, copper contours of five slugs nosing out of the chambers. He knew the sixth lay unseen in front of the hammer. The weapon was clean and well oiled. 'Webley' stood out in raised letters above the handle. The initial coolness of the metal was already warming under his touch. He sighed with relief then yawned, to his surprise, a deep, satisfying yawn. The tension that had made his palms damp and his throat dry lifted with the heft of the pistol and the bite of the grip against his palm.

Okay, he thought, you don't want to shoot anybody, but you gotta be ready. You gotta strike first. Uncle John was with him now. He always said: hit first, hit hard, and hit when they least expect it. He had drummed this into

Pat by word and deed and taught him how to fight dirty. Now, the lessons made sense. Pat stuck the gun in his waistband and covered it with the flap of his uniform blouse.

He waited. He felt some confidence now because not only did he have the Webley, he also had surprise on his side. He watched as the old woman rose with difficulty from her rocker, looked his way, and entered the house. Shortly thereafter a young girl opened the door, jumped off the porch, and ran full speed toward the truck. Her thin arms and legs pumped like pistons and her long auburn hair danced to the rhythm of her steps and reflected the late afternoon light. She wore a short-sleeved cotton dress.

"Mah Grandma Velma says fer you to come inside and eat," she said from a safe distance.

"Tell her thank you then," said Pat. "I'm coming."

The girl turned and sprinted to the house. Pat followed her, adjusting his gait to accommodate the barrel of the pistol in his belt and glancing down several times to be sure the handle did not bulge suspiciously under his uniform. He climbed the porch steps and knocked. The young girl opened the door and stepped back. Behind her sat Velma and a younger woman Pat assumed was Velma's daughter. He nodded a greeting and stood self-consciously with his hands clasped in front of him over the pistol.

"You come right on in," the grandmother said. "Set yoursef down at the table. You hungry?" The aroma of biscuits and ham and the popping sound of eggs frying made him aware of how hungry he was.

"Yes, ma'am."

He sat at the crude table in the warmth of the fireplace and ate biscuits, fried eggs, and grits awash in butter and sprinkled with salt and pepper. The young girl whispered to her mother, ran out the back door, and returned with an RC Cola, which she placed before him. While he ate, the women watched him, observing a curiosity they might never see again in their valley. He felt no threat and even forgot his predicament momentarily as he savored the food and company. After eating, he thanked them repeatedly and finally managed to ask, "By the way, where's Oren?"

"He's out in the smokehouse with the men folk," the young girl said before either of the women could answer. Each looked at her rather sternly, and she smiled as if she knew she had done wrong but could not be rebuked in his presence.

Buoyed by the pistol and his presence among women, Pat said, "What're they doing out there?"

"Oh, never you mind about them," Velma said quickly. "Oren won't be long."

"Well, I sure do appreciate your hospitality," Pat said again. Thinking it safest to avoid facing four men at once, he said, "I'll just wait for Oren in the truck."

As he stepped out onto the front porch, he saw them standing near a shed. Two had shotguns. One held his in the crook of his arm with the barrel pointed at the ground. The other stood like a crucifix, pressing the long gun against the back of his neck, one wrist draped over the barrel, the other over the stock. All four watched Pat walk to the truck. Then three of them turned and entered the smokehouse. Just before ducking through the low door the

last man spun, fluid as a cat, raised his shotgun to his shoulder and *click, click* the hammers hit the empty chambers sending two echoes into the twilight sky.

Oren angled toward the truck. "Where you goin', Chaw? You fixin' to drive off in mah truck?"

"No, sir. Just fixin' to wait for you to come back."

"You ain't got much more waitin' to do. Ah almost got you to where you're goin'," Oren said as he started the old gray truck.

Pat could feel his stomach tighten again as they drove away. 'Gotta be ready,' he thought. Oren's headlights bore into the descending darkness, and Pat fortified himself for whatever was to come. He felt heavy with food and fatigue. Night came on, the motor purred; the truck swayed and rocked him to a rhythm that carried him away.

"Last stop, Chaw. Wake up, boy."

Pat heard the voice, but could not locate it. He struggled toward it, past the clutches of his dreams, holding his breath.

"What? Where are we?"

"London, boy. Right in the middle of her. Ah figured ah'd take you all the way."

They had stopped in front of a two-story house. Pat looked out at a hand-lettered sign: *Lodgers Welcome*. A smaller sign swung in the wind below it: *Proprietor Richard Bragg*.

"Reckon you kin git some real sleep tonight here to Rick's. You look like you need it. Now, hop on out and don't forgit your kit bag."

Still barely awake, Pat descended from the cab, pulled his bag from the pickup bed, and glanced back at Oren

31

through the open passenger door. With two fingers the mountaineer fished into a narrow pocket in the bib of his overalls and pulled out some bills rolled tightly into the shape and length of a cigarette.

"This here's fer you," he said extending the money to Pat.

"What's this?" Pat said, taking the roll.

"Forty bucks."

"But...what for?"

"It's fer you, Chaw, seein' as how you're servin' fer all of us. Probably hep you along your way. Matthew, Howard, and them boys in Blue Hole chipped in too."

Oren reached across the seat, pulled the passenger door closed, and u-turned on the narrow residential street. As he pulled away into the night raising his index finger from atop the steering wheel, Pat felt a sharp jab from the Webley in his stomach.

~~~

Sue watched him intently for a time after he finished his story. "I'm going to go make you a pie," she said finally. "That'll make you feel better." She leaned forward and extended her hand. Pat took it and searched her eyes. "I'm so glad you told me," she said. "It'll make you feel better, even better than pie."

"What kind are you going to make?"

THE DANCER

An Alluring Memory

She floats up the gangplank like a strand of silk on light air; her dancer's carriage, elegant yet arrogant, casts a cautionary spell; her blue-black hair, sleek and severe, is drawn tight to a bun; her bare, olive-toned arms and feathery hands alight occasionally on the handrails for balance. An offshore breeze wafting up the ship's hull lifts her skirts as she places a toe on deck and long fingers on the first officer's extended forearm. Her dark eyes barely acknowledge his reflexive glance at her thighs or his welcome aboard. A man, observing this theater from a deck above, wonders, then shakes his head and lets it fall to his chest. No need watching the mule train of passengers who follow. She was what he had hoped to see.

When they were first married, Jeannie accompanied Jackson on his 'Croesus cruises,' as she called them, because in their youth these voyages seemed so lavish. They ate and drank free, lounged in the sun, and grooved on the music into the wee hours, he perched atop a collapsible chair driving the band, laying down the beat, she draped over a bar stool filtering out the real deals, who were few, from the barflies, who were many. She had learned that some men, off on vacation from their families,

believed cruise ships to be full of opportunities, so she was ready for them. "Did your wife have to stay home to work?" Jeannie would ask when she spotted a pale halo on a ring finger. Jeannie loved to ambush the philanderers, to jab them with questions about their infidelity, and Jackson knew why.

She had shared the dark secret with him the night they became engaged – after smoking a ritual joint or two. She told him she had once seen her father with her mother's best friend, Mrs. Villatoro, half-naked on the tendril-patterned cushions of the squeaky back porch swing. "I was only ten, for God's sake," she said. "I was collecting leaves for a Girl Scout badge in the woods behind Auntie V's house." The writhing bodies had stunned her, she said, dropped her flat on her stomach. They had fascinated but repulsed her. She remembered being well camouflaged in her scout uniform but still feared being seen, so she lay low and still until Auntie V moaned and giggled and they went inside holding hands.

"I've never breathed a word of this to anyone," she whispered to Jackson, "hoping my silence would erase the memory, but of course it hasn't." Instead, she found that the rhythmic squeak of a pump handle, the earthy smells of her garden, even things unidentifiable could fling her back across time where she could smell the dirt again and feel the pine needles pricking her chest as she tried not to look at her father's fleshy white ass.

"Our life was never the same," she said. Jackson held her hand as she recalled the silence that encroached on their household and her parents' disengagement from their intimate dances: their teasing, their private

nicknames, the ease of their co-existence, all congealed in the chill that summer, then disappeared. "My damned Dad! He must have been discovered." Jeannie whispered.

"And what happened to Auntie V?" Jackson asked.

"Oh God! She died six years later on her cellar stairs. Rumor had it that she missed the second step from the bottom, fell backward, and snapped her neck on a riser – never moved a muscle after the fall. My Mom went to her service, but my Dad didn't."

To Jeannie's guilty relief, Auntie V's death released her. The wicked witch was dead; her spell, broken. "I couldn't shout hooray from the rooftops, but I did begin to feel better. Then, a little later, I discovered I could sing," she said, brightening at the memory. This was a natural love affair, her mother told her. The musical genes of her maternal grandmother, a graduate of Juilliard, had survived, leapt a generation, and spawned in Jeannie's pool. At seventeen she had a smoky contralto voice, a broken heart, and perfect pitch, nice credentials for a blues singer.

She learned about phrasing, breath control and interpretation, but mostly she just sang...during long teenage showers, in the car, and with a jazz group on weekends. In college she got into minor keys, dissonance, and syncopation, sounds and off beats that reflected the lack of resolution at home. She found when she sang from the heart, allowing the loneliness she felt to prevail, she could hush and haunt a room, but she was unwilling to do that often. "It makes me feel vulnerable," she told Jackson.

"When I first heard you sing," he said, "I was touched almost to tears. It's one of my most memorable moments

in music. I even remember what you said when I introduced myself to you after that set. You were still revved from the applause and you said, 'Yeah, I know you. You play so clean. I love your music, man.'"

~~~

"*Hombre, me encanta la musica.*" He heard the husky voice that night on the cruise ship as he returned to the bandstand. Even before he was able to associate it with the woman he had watched float across the gangplank that afternoon, he realized her first words to him had the same meaning as the first words Jeannie had spoken to him years ago.

Drummers pick up on rhythms like this. The lapping of waves, a woodpecker's vamp, the swaying of hips. If it's repetitive, there's a rhythm. Jackson returned to her table when they finished playing. "*Buenas noches,*" he said, pulling up an extra chair and placing it off her shoulder so she had to turn away from the two couples sharing her table. He wanted no interference. "Jackson," he said, extending his hand. *Me llamo Jackson* – that's my name – and that's the end of my Spanish. *No mas* he smiled.

"Well, *no te preocupes, Yackson.* Don't worry. I speak English and I do love *la musica.* You can really touch your toes to it."

"Yeah, it's toe touching music all right. May I ask where you are from?"

"I am from Madrid," she said, thickening the first 'd' and softening the second to a 'th'. "It is a city *muy, muy bonita* and *llena de vida*, full of life." She had lived life fully, perhaps too fully, Jackson thought, aware that this up-close impression was at odds with the apparition he

had seen from afar that afternoon. But she sat, even half-turned in her chair, as she walked, buoyant, diaphanous, her posture in perfect plumb. In contrast to her lightness of limb, her face was somber, more Moorish than Latin. It was marked along the jawline by a trail of pocks, the vestige of an adolescence long past. The eyes were private, not-to-be-trifled-with eyes. They looked down a flat, broad-bridged nose that gave strength not beauty to her face.

Jackson took a chance. "Goya would have loved your face," he said.

"Goya?"

"Yeah, the Spanish painter," Jackson replied with the hint of a question in his voice. Did she not know him? "I'm not an expert, but I think he painted some Spanish royalty when he was young ... before he got consumed with disaster and pestilence. I remember some portraits in the Prado Museum in Madrid, great faces."

"*Ah, sí. Goya. Perdoneme,* but I didn't understand your pronunciation. You have visited *el Prado*?"

"Yes, I have. I was touring with Dr. John. Maybe you've heard of him. We played Madrid, Barcelona, and Seville. Didn't have much free time, but I did go to the Prado. Loved it," he said with emphasis.

"*El Prado es una maravilla,*" she said. "It is 'a marvelous,' right?"

"We would say it is 'a marvel', but I agree, *es una maravilla, correcto?*"

She smiled at this linguistic somersault, a minor amusement. The smile rolled gently over her grave features forming fine crinkles at the corners of her eyes,

soothing their intensity. It softened the set of her jaw and the vibe between them. Jackson returned the smile. It worked, he thought, like flowers on a week night. "Would you like to buy me a drink, Yackson?"

When she rose to leave almost an hour later, she extended her hand toward his lips in a courtly, antiquated custom. Jackson, caught off guard, reacted by catching her hand in both of his, a response grooved in his brain since his days as a Little League shortstop. Then, looking into her eyes, pleading for some small signal that he was not making a fool of himself, he bent and bestowed a misdirected kiss on her watch. "*Buenas noches,*" he said, unable to stifle a grin. "Ah, my dear Yackson," she said in her throaty voice, her hard Spanish eyes softening again, "Good night."

~~~

"*Ah, my dear Yackson.*" He could still hear it. A come hither farewell if he ever heard one. But what the hell are you doing, Jackson thought, slumped across the only chair in his steerage cabin. Leave her alone!

His mood, as often occurred after he had played well and hard, was losing altitude, letting down through the clouds of adrenaline and nervous energy. Playing drums could alter his mind. Maintaining a clean, relentless beat, hands and feet creating their own catchy embellishments, bearing down then easing back for contrast, tapping out accented triplets on the snare's sweet spot, then only on the rim or on a wood block, mouth involuntarily askew, then a Rich-type roll, left left, right right, slowly accelerating until the sticks are a blur, and the applause spontaneous: all this could leave him high. But afterward,

off-stage and alone, he would sink to reality again. Jeannie called it 'rubbing the rosy off his glasses.' He thought of her and told himself again, Let it go, man. This lady of Spain ain't worth it.

As the lusty glow of their youth cooled over the years, Jeannie had become the ballast in his inconstant life, a shelter from the craziness of the music world. She had given up her singing because singing the blues gave her the blues. She often left the stage not only sad, but even angry. "You know," she told Jackson once driving home from a late night gig, "I don't blame Frankie one little bit for shooting Johnnie, the little shit. He deserved it." Jackson took note – a father's influence can last a lifetime. He did not argue the point.

The less she sang, the more she engaged in Jackson's career, booking his dates, negotiating his contracts, jumping on problems with the purpose of a pit bull. She was good at it, tough and knowledgeable and yet accommodating to other musicians' agents, as long as they kept their word. One lie, though, one false promise and she wrote them off.

"You know," he said to her one night as they were drifting off to sleep, "you make me feel protected."

"How's that?"

"You make me feel 'safe and sound' like my mom used to say."

"Hmm...love you," she said wiggling backward into him.

~ ~ ~

The sense of security he felt nestled next to her never waned. "Hey, J, whatdaya say?" became the opening line

39

of his almost daily calls to her when he was on the road. Whether he was sitting backstage in a theater in Nashville or killing time in a park in San Francisco on tour with Clapton or Toussaint or someone else, she was always with him. When he miscalculated a time difference and woke her, she never asked him to call back.

And she was always on his mind when he succumbed to temptation. Tipsy girls and women, enchanted by the music or by musicians, chatted him up, offered their favors, hustled him off to the most unlikely venues: a tanning salon once, a surprisingly spacious bunk in the cab of an 18-wheeler, a leather sofa in the office of a state legislator in Bismarck, North Dakota. But, plodding back to his rooms in the middle of the night, he always felt despicable and puzzled over why he repeatedly did this.

He would lie on the bed in his hotel and call home. The calls became a ritual, a salve to soothe his guilt. They would chat and laugh and he would tell her he loved her and before falling asleep he would recite the litany to himself: it really meant nothing; it was a harmless occupational hazard; he was not – never had been – even vaguely interested in an affair; and, Jeannie was not hurt by these one night stands because she never knew about them, thank God! These obedient sheep jumped out of their stalls when summoned and trotted docilely across his conscience – each bearing a piece of wooly truth – until he fell asleep.

It was true; the women meant nothing to him. He could remember venues better than faces or personalities. But thoughts about the other truth, his carousing, taunted him. Risking everything for nothing made no sense. He

wondered if it were an addiction like Booker and heroin, or some cryptic compulsion to prove something or to wreck his marriage. He had no answers. His only certainty was that eventually his infidelities would cripple their marriage. Even if he could keep Jeannie in the dark, he knew he could wreck it all by himself. Pushing up from his chair, he pulled off his clothes and slid into bed. I do this simply because I can, he concluded, as he lay his head on the pillow. If I can do it, I can stop doing it. I've just gotta kick this habit! *Ah yes, my dear Yackson, you really must.*

~~~

He was wading in flotsam, pants rolled up tight below the knees, strangling the calves. God, they ached. The feet were numb in icy water, but he waded on through construction debris: a saw, its teeth bared, a yellow crime scene tape, and twine, yards and yards of it, snarling his ankles, impeding his progress. Doggedly he pushed on toward a grand pavilion and the music. Gypsy chants, Sephardic, hoarse voices in minor keys, the percussion of stamping feet drawing him into deeper water. She drifted vaporously toward him across wooden boards, topless, back arched imperiously, fierce eyes locked on his. Her many hands and flexed wrists swayed above her head like October branches while her fingers made chestnuts click and snap, embellishing the perfect accented triplets rolling off her feet.

"I dreamed about you last night," Jackson said stretching out on a deck chair next to hers.

"I am flattered." She spoke without turning her face from the sun. The tell in her eyes was unreadable behind her extravagant sunglasses. "A woman does not appear in

a man's dreams without reason, you know, and a man does not tell a woman he dreams of her without reason *tampoco*." The conversation had accelerated from zero to sixty in a bat of her hidden lashes. "I trust it was a pleasant dream."

"I dreamed you were dancing the flamenco in a grand pavilion on the water somewhere," he said, "and that your footwork was much better than my drumming."

She turned from the sun, abandoning her tanning devotion, and slowly removed her sunglasses to look at him. The eyes were hard again, suspicious.

"Is this a joke?"

"No. Why do you ask?"

"I *did* dance flamenco in Sevilla on the Mediterranean."

"Is Sevilla on the Mediterranean?" he asked.

"Wherever! But how do you know this if you even don't know my name?" She had coyly declined to give Jackson her name the previous night, even after he bought her a third drink and teased her about being mysterious.

"If we are going to discuss your presence in my dreams, such an intimate topic, I must first know your name," he said.

"For now you may call me Marquesa." She returned to the cover of her sunglasses and looked away from him back into the sun.

"Marquesa. How wonderful! I am conversing with royalty. I knew it," he said to flatter her. Then, so as not to surrender too much leverage, "Or was that your stage name?"

"Ah, Yackson, you are the drummer from heaven, but you have a mean stripe. No, my name is Charlotta Ruiz Rosa, La Marquesa de Girona y Bourbon," she said in concession. "That is my full name and *titulo*, which you will not remember I'm sure. *Ahora*, tell me how you know I was a dancer of flamenco."

Jackson studied her. He saw tawny skin, probably protected from Spain's harsh sun and pampered; sinewy arms, veins tracing subtly around her biceps and down her forearms; muscular legs even in repose; luxuriant, raven-black hair, probably its natural color and a source of pride. It flew in the sea air, freed from its usual sleek discipline. Only the hands, willowy but worn, hinted at her age; mauve squiggles meandered across the long bones running out from wrists to knuckles. She had wrapped herself in a sheer pareu, orange and teal with black and white, open-mouthed fish, nibbling here and there and seeming to swim across the folds of the material as it rippled with the breeze. A small Macy's tag flapped occasionally from a corner at her knee. She had tucked the garment into itself a discreet two inches above the nipple line. Not high fashion, Jackson thought, not expensive. She wore no jewelry, not even a ring, perhaps because she seemed to be sunbathing conscientiously. Every inch of skin glistened with an oil smelling of bananas; she had positioned her deck chair perpendicular to the sun, and angled her limbs and face for maximum exposure. She turned her head and flipped her arms at regular intervals for even basting. Jackson thought: she is around fifty, hard working, disciplined, and physically active because she is quite fit for her age; she is organized, and calculating, but

not wealthy or well educated. Had Jeannie been there, she would have given Jackson good marks for his insights, but he knew her observations would have been more refined and insightful than his. Her keen intuition gave her an edge over Jackson in this little game they often played.

"I *didn't* know you were a dancer," Jackson said. "How could I have known?"

"That is your secret apparently."

"My dear Marquesa, my dream makes perfect sense. You look like a dancer. You move like a dancer. You are Spanish, as is flamenco. I had just spent one hour flirting with you. Then I go to sleep and dream of you dancing. *Por favor*, is that not logical? Now tell me, how did you become the beautiful dancer you are?"

"I will tell you on one condition."

"Anything. I will do anything you ask."

"Invite me to lunch, my dear Yackson."

~ ~ ~

Lunch became a ritual, a rite of passage Jackson hoped. It was always late and long, Spanish style. Jackson ate absentmindedly and he fell under her spell. She ate with finesse, European style, her graceful left hand holding the fork inverted and ever so lightly, while her right hand, using her heavy dinner knife with the dexterity of a surgeon, sliced and diced and arranged delicate bites on the fork. Jackson admired her flair just as he admired hands sweeping a keyboard or dancing between frets, but it was the quantity of food she consumed that fascinated him, astonished him really. At every lunch she prepared lady-like portions of every offering on the buffet table: soup, cold or hot; green salad, fruit salad, pasta salad;

meat, fish, and chicken entrées; breads and crackers with butter and dips; each luscious dessert and coffee, black. And, she showed no signs of appreciation, satiation, or self-consciousness. The food was there. It was included in the fare, so she ate. Peculiar, Jackson thought. It's like she doesn't get enough at home.

"I was a prodigy," she began. "In my region of Andalusia to study flamenco was an option in my private *colegio* – I think that is like your high school. It is part of our *cultura,* so I was drawn to it. Plus, I wanted to avoid swimming or bow shooting. No interest, *nada.* I was a natural, my teacher said, and I adored it." She paused to convey an artful arrangement of salmon, capers, and dill to her lips.

"So, you continued after high school?"

"I continued *in* high school. I was sent to a school of dance in Sevilla. I had the best teachers and trainers and, of course, I worked at it every day," she said with no accent at all.

"Do you still dance?"

"Ah, my dear Yackson..." she hesitated and looked into the distance, promoting a wistful silence. "I dance in my room every day."

Dancers are actors, Jackson remembered reading. This was certainly true of the Marquesa. She was drama itself. She could summon a coquettish character with a bat of her lashes or a sensual turn of her shoulder, and then dismiss her with the cool tone of a single word, but Jackson found her transformations unsettling. He preferred Jeannie's straight-talk. She always calls them the way she sees them, he thought as his attention returned to

the Marquesa. "Do you mean that literally, that you dance in your room?" he asked her.

"I mean I no longer dance for *el publico*. I dance for myself. I had a great following, especially in the south of Spain, but that story is for another time, my dear," she said tipping the last drops from her *café solo*.

"As you wish, but remember, you have promised to continue. We play from 9 to 1 tonight. Perhaps over a drink afterwards?"

"*Vamos a ver*," she said, "we shall see."

She did appear that evening at about 10 o'clock, early by Spanish standards, dressed simply in black and without much jewelry. She sat at an empty table. Jackson acknowledged her from the bandstand with a big American smile. She responded curiously by laying an index finger on her temple. Maybe it's a Spanish gesture, Jackson thought, meaning 'I see you, I caught your greeting.' Later, two gentlemen joined her, seating themselves close to her, one on each side. Surrounded. Jeannie could have handled them, he thought. Three drinks arrived and from Jackson's distant perspective conversation flowed. Another round, open-mouthed laughter, but no dancing. His attention flickered between the table pantomime he was trying to interpret and the pulse he was feeling through the drums; table to traps, traps to table as if there were a pulsating strobe in the room. He looked up once to find the Marquesa and one of the gentlemen had gone. They did not return during the break, but reappeared as the band began its last set.

Jeannie did not go away though; she lingered in his thoughts. He wondered how often *he* was in *her* thoughts

and if she had liaisons too. She was a free spirit, after all, and he was on the road often. As he beat out a lively tempo on the drums, his imagination swept him down a dangerous slope. The loneliness of her life in New York certainly could make her vulnerable to some smooth operator and living in a metropolis, shit... her afternoon trysts in fancy hotels would be practically undetectable. God, her life was made to order for infidelity, just as his was! Clapping suddenly shattered his fantasy. The set was finished. He heard the increase in applause when the piano player called his name and he responded with a riff that plunged them back into the chorus of their last song. The audience loved it, but Jackson said 'fuck me' under his breath.

~~~

Ten minutes later Jackson approached her table. She was alone again. As she gestured for him to sit beside her, he took her hand and dusted a kiss upon it. "See, I'm learning, getting better."

"To be authentic, my dear Yackson, you never touch your lips to the hand," she instructed. "Also not to the cheeks." Jackson smiled; her accent made 'lips' sound like 'leaps'; it almost rhymed with cheeks. "Sadly, you kiss only the air...or the lips," she added as an afterthought. "Lips are for lips" (leaps are for leaps), she instructed. Zero to sixty again, he thought.

Perhaps the red wine she drank that night inverted her sense of modesty or put her inhibitions at bay. Whatever it did, as promised, she rolled out the dream-like tale of her career. It was full of gypsies, handsome guitar players, rapid passages of music and lovers, scarlet and black

47

scandal, castanets and minarets and, above all, *el baile,* as she always referred to the flamenco. It was set in the clubs and theaters of Cadiz, Seville and Malaga with an occasional performance before royalty in Madrid. Jackson ordered her another Rioja at last call. They remained alone as the bar closed around them, but the Marquesa was undeterred. She had been a star, she said, at least among those in Spain who were aficionados of *el baile.* She had twice danced for the King, had a fling with a bullfighter, a fight with the tax authorities, and a marriage to the Marques de Girona. Jackson, a son of White River Junction, Vermont, sat sipping a beer, listening and imagining: the smoky bars and plush theaters of Andalusia, Spain itself, hot and exotic, and this sultry, suspicious woman, who had loved and labored and been a part of it all. It made him feel as if he had spent his life in a monastery. Then, as quickly as she had begun her story, she stopped. "Walk me home, my dear Yackson. I have had too much Rioja. I have a headache and must sleep. *Por favor,*" she said warmly, smiling briefly and sliding her hand into the crook of his arm. When they reached the lobby, she kissed him on the neck below the ear and lightly descended the stairway to her cabin.

~~~

Their brief song was a rhapsody, irregular and improvised during the last days of the cruise – deck chair rendezvous, lunches winding through the past but skirting the moment, solitary siestas, and Courvoisier after midnight. They were in sync and yet a covetous tension hummed between them. He could not find the key to free her – for more than a delightful moment now and then –

from the protected preserve she seemed to prefer. He was inhibited by her presence and her exotic past. Her title and poses jostled his instincts, made him feel gullible and green. One minute she would raise the veil, soften her eyes, place a hand on his, and listen as he told her risqué tales of the music world, onstage and off. *No me digas –* you don't say – she would exclaim kittenishly. The next minute she would look away and the veil would rise again, eyes wary, her hand withdrawn and cool on the sweaty surface of a glass. In neither persona did she ask Jackson about his life outside music. Jeannie would have. She used to find out all there was to know about her onboard hustlers. But the Marquesa was indifferent to his biography. Perhaps, by refraining from asking about his personal life, she meant to keep the door to hers well shut. Jackson could dig that. Their no-pry agreement was keeping her a safe distance from his world too, but it was also keeping him from her cabin.

Time was running out. Jackson knew the Marquesa held all the cards and had put him into an alien role. He had always played the part of the hunted, which he felt he had mastered; he was never the hunter, which he was learning required much more skill. As he wandered back to his cabin it occurred to him that the closer he came to being rejected, the more he wanted the Marquesa. Denial and desire, linked so irreconcilably. What a shame, he thought, as he stepped into his cabin alone.

~~~

"So what's life like in Espana these days, for royalty that is?" he asked one morning as they lay sunning on a lee deck.

49

"Are you really interested in that? We are not full of surprises. We have our affairs and scandals like every people. We just do them on a grander scale and we are discovered by paparazzi. Nothing stays a secret for long," she said from behind her large sunglasses.

"Well, tell me a secret, Mata Hari. What is the King really like? Do you know him?"

"I have met him, the first time with my husband and mother. The second time, thirteen months later, he approached me, called me by name, and asked after my mother. I was impressed. Of course, some magazines say that he is a ladies' man, that he has, as you say, a wondering eye."

"Wandering eye, Marquesa, although he probably is wondering too."

"Oh, my dear Yackson, I tell you the Prince is the fox. He has the Queen's looks, her mannerisms, her interests in the arts and fashion. He is a lovely boy." As she spoke, Jackson admired her contours and imperial profile, canted precisely toward the sun. Her chest with its sheen of fruity oil rose and fell, twice for every roll of the ship. "I would love you to rub some lotion on my shoulders and back," she said as she rolled over.

"Do you know New York City?" he asked as he began to rub.

"Why would you ask that?" she said casually, but he felt the muscles tense in her neck.

"Just wondering." He allowed a long pause to widen between them; he wanted her to answer. "I work there often," he said finally, preferring not to disclose that he

actually lived there, and paused again for her response. "Just curious."

The Marquesa waited several beats. "Curiosity can kill the *gatito*."

"Curiosity is also responsible for advances in science, the arts, and many other human endeavors," he said as he slipped the straps of her bathing suit from her lean shoulders to apply more lotion.

She rolled over again, swung her toned legs to the side and faced Jackson nose to nose. He could feel her breath; a stray hair tickled his forehead. "*Hombre*," she said, "you are not now thinking of advancing science."

"I always favor progress, Marquesa. The slower we move, the more we lose." He said these words semi-seriously while staring at his reflection in her dark glasses. While her eyes were hidden, her lips betrayed an expression of amusement, he thought, or perhaps acquiescence, but his unspoken question remained unanswered.

~~~

The entertainment director radiated an astringent lime fragrance. He stood too close when he conversed and his busy hands were constantly plucking a hair from someone's collar or stroking his goatee. He had been touting the Grande Finale of the cruise for a week. Surf and turf served late, champagne on the house, formal dress optional, and gaiety – lots of gaiety. The band would play an hour later than usual, which curtailed Jackson's ultimate opportunity with the Marquesa and irked him generally. With each cruise he grew to hate these tinselly nights more. The counterfeit hilarity, the requests for

schmaltz like *MacArthur Park* and *Muskrat Love,* the passengers' slurred compliments. The Finals used to drive Jeannie nuts so she took to her cabin early.

The Marquesa did her one better; she never even appeared for it. He kept looking up throughout the long evening hoping to see her quirky, index-finger-to-temple greeting or to watch her effortless glide through the room. Damn, he thought, she's stiffing me on our last night. He banged away at the music, sticks becoming heavier, finesse vaporizing in the heat of his labor. Finally, they arrived at *The Party's Over.* He gave out a long sigh with his final flourish.

Minutes later he waved off his usual, a draught beer the bartender started to draw for him, and asked for a scotch instead. "Tough night, Jackson?"

"Yeah. Too much Lester Lanin shit, man. I gotta get back to the City." A moment later watching the man's deft hands punctuate a bright blue drink with a paper umbrella Jackson asked, "You seen the Marquesa tonight?"

"She was here couple hours ago, but I was too busy to chat."

"One more, Phil. Make it a double," Jackson said, lifting his empty glass. He shoved back from the bar, grabbed his new drink, and stepped out on deck to feel the soft caress of Caribbean air one last time. He unbuttoned his sweaty collar, took off his shoes, and watched the moon slip behind an amethyst cloud. In time the moonlight and drink lifted the persistent tension of hope and allowed Jackson to consider his failed quest. He did not want to make excuses, but the Marquesa's whims and moodiness had thrown him off. She had escaped because

he had never known precisely whom he was courting. But now he could return to Jeannie a chaste man. This was a good thing, a legitimate clean start. 'This Could Be the Start of Something New' popped into his head. He hummed a few bars and stepped lightly down the passageway feeling like Gene Kelly.

~~~

"There you are, my dear Yackson." The husky voice flew at him from behind like a brick. He froze for an instant, a snapshot of a walker in full stride.

"Jesus, where have you been, Marquesa? What are you doing down here?"

"*Querido*, – my dear – you are upset. Please don't be. I passed my last evening on the deck," she said. "So lovely, the sounds of the sea, the moonlight. I just preferred that to the *ruido* where you were. Sorry." As she spoke, her long fingers produced a key from beneath her shawl. "Isn't it fatal that we should meet by chance on our last night?" she asked. Moving gracefully in front of him she led him up several stairwells and down a passageway. Finally she stopped in front of her door, inserted her key, and held her door open for him. "Do you believe in fate, my dear Yackson?"

His first step into her tiny cabin scattered his thoughts of chastity and redemption like butterflies. That step was his answer to her question, his acceptance of her invitation. He stood shoes in hand, slightly tipsy from the scotch, as she rose on tiptoe, kissed him with moistened lips, then knelt before him and laid his shoes on the floor.

Shortly before dawn he rolled out of their narrow berth. "Be back at ten," he whispered, "so we can have coffee before we disembark. Okay? Do you hear me?"

"Hmmm."

At ten o'clock he returned to find her door ajar. "*Buenos dias,*" he called. No answer. He pushed in tentatively. No Marquesa. No baggage. Only his shoes on the pillow. In one he found a rolled piece of stationery. Slumped wearily on the bed, he unscrolled it expecting an explanation or a word of farewell, but there below the ship's name was the Marquesa's theatrical adieu: a scarlet imprint of her lips. He held it for a full minute then let it fall to the floor.

As the months and years passed he discovered that she had left him more than a lipstick smudge. Memories remained, drifting like phantom companions along the edges of his mind. Why did they linger when memories of the others had escaped and vanished? It was not the love making that kept her there; their night had been nothing special. So, then it was the grace with which she moved that had cast such an enduring spell and her exotic story and the blush of theater she managed to daub on everything she touched. And yet, he reluctantly admitted, it was more than that; it was the sense of unease moving among those memories, a nagging impurity; it was a suspicion that he had been willingly duped that haunted him still.

A Flawed Farewell

Several women descend from a Maids R Us van and,

hunched against a gritty, winter wind sweeping down First Avenue, scurry toward a nearby bus stop. As they approach, a man stares vacantly out the window of a deli. He is preoccupied with thoughts of his recent separation, but irresistibly his attention is drawn to one of the women. She is bundled, wool cap pulled down, collar turned up, listing slightly under the weight of a Macy's bag, but still she moves effortlessly – like a dancer. Involuntarily the man rises from his chair, staring. The woman glides to a halt in line to board her bus. As she turns her back to the wind, the dark eyes, unprepared, glance through the deli window. The man races the length of the deli, then down the sidewalk but the procession of dirty windows and billboards is already filing slowly by him into traffic. Awash in fumes and breathless, he spots her face again in the last window, an index finger lifting curiously to her temple.

SWEET CONFUSION

Mickey did not want his wife Elizabeth to intrude on him at a crucial moment, so he decided to wait until 8:30 a.m. She would be in her office at 8:30 because it opened then and she was pathologically punctual. She had a twenty-minute walk to work so she left at 8 o'clock sharp daily.

Having said goodbye to her at the front door, Mickey lay down on the sofa to wait. He dozed off reading the comics, awoke at 9:15, poured himself a first coffee, and took his last doughnut from his secret stash in the broom closet. Ready at last, he went to the bedroom, pulled open his sock drawer, and removed two jars of garlic powder hidden in a pair of thick rolled up athletic socks.

Mickey was not the type to analyze where ideas come from. He saw himself as an artist, not an intellectual. He had said as much as a high school sophomore. That year he had led a cow up three flights of stairs and onto the high school roof. Theoretically, Mickey calculated, getting the cow down would prove much more difficult than leading her up. To his relief, theory proved to be reality. After sixteen hours of unsuccessful coaxing, a veterinarian anesthetized her; and the Fire Department, with the help of a moving company, lowered her over the side of the school building in a jury-rigged sling.

Mickey became a legend. It changed not only his reputation but also his perception of himself, and he reveled in his new status. He worked to perpetuate it and had some success so that even now, seven years later, people asked him about it.

He also became an odds-on favorite to be suspended from school. When the principal asked him why he put the cow on the roof, Mickey was genuinely flummoxed.

"Why?" he asked. "I really have no idea, Mr. Briley." Then, as if he had just discovered something about himself he said, "I never ask myself 'why.'"

"Why not?" the principal asked.

Mickey shrugged and said, "I don't know ... maybe because there's never an answer to those big 'why' questions. The fact is, nobody knows why I did it." Mr. Briley said nothing. Mickey, uncomfortable with the silence, adjusted himself in the chair and so as not to appear obstinate or insolent he added, "I do ask myself the 'how' questions though."

His current project supported this extemporaneous self-assessment. Its genius lay in how simple, fast, and inexpensive it was to set it up in comparison with how long it would produce results. Mickey figured set-up would take ten minutes and, with luck, the project could run productively for weeks, even months. He all but rubbed his hands in glee as he placed the jars of garlic powder on a shelf above the sink in the bathroom.

He returned to the bedroom and took a photo with his phone of Elizabeth's talcum powder jar surrounded by her other toiletries. He needed to be able to reposition it precisely where he had found it. Elizabeth was meticulous

and a creature of habit. If something were even slightly out of place, she would notice it and, in the very least, become suspicious. He carefully lifted the squat, glass vase from its place on her dressing table, carried it to the bathroom, and placed it next to the jars of garlic powder on the shelf.

With all the ingredients in place, Mickey took a breath and relaxed for a moment. His thoughts went back to an afternoon one month ago. Elizabeth had been preparing spaghetti sauce in their kitchen and he had been sipping a Coke, munching on chips, and trying to be helpful.

"Oh shoot," she said coming out of the pantry. "I'm out of garlic cloves." Elizabeth cooked strictly by the book. If a recipe called for four pounds of tomatoes she would not simply throw in four or five tomatoes; she would cut them in pieces and weigh them on her food scale until she had precisely four pounds.

"Use garlic powder instead," Mickey, her sous-chef, suggested. He cooked instinctively, a pinch of salt here, a dash of horseradish there. "Go ahead," he said, when he saw her reluctance. "Live dangerously."

"Oh, alright," she agreed, but she was not comfortable with the substitution or the imprecision.

It was a mundane moment. Little wonder Mickey had not thought of it again for a month. When he did, he and Elizabeth were moving silently through their well-worn morning routine. Elizabeth showered while Mickey made their coffee. Mickey returned to their little bedroom, which was flooded with spring sunshine that morning, and placed Elizabeth's coffee on her dressing table just as she came out of the bathroom wrapped in a towel. He then got back in bed and read her headlines and newsy anecdotes

while she sipped her coffee, did her hair and make-up, and daubed a drop of Chanel No. 5 behind each ear – her mother's influence. She cherished these moments. Her efforts made her look and feel professional, ready for her workday, and Mickey's presence gave her ritual a touch of intimacy, a quality that, sadly, was missing in their marriage. Her last ablution before dressing was to draw forth a powder puff from its jar and, tapping it expertly, send a light cloud of scented talc falling across her chest.

Mickey watched her in the dressing table mirror as the talc fell gently on her skin and she watched him, but that spring morning she noticed an expression on his face she had never seen before. By a most improbable coincidence of timing, Elizabeth was witnessing one of her husband's eureka moments. Innocently present at the birth of his idea, she slipped on her clothes and was on her way to work.

"That was a whole month ago," Mickey reminded himself. "No time to dally." With that, he turned his attention to the task before him. He unscrewed the silver top of the talc jar, took the puff out, and placed it carefully in the inverted top so as not to leave traces of talc on the sink. Working carefully, he withdrew a plastic zip-lock bag from his breast pocket and poured the talc from its jar into the bag. Finally, Mickey poured almost two jars of garlic powder into the talc jar. He was surprised and delighted that the color and consistency of the garlic powder so closely matched the talc. Then he put the puff back in the jar and worked it down into the powder. It sat comfortably in its new nest as if it had been there for years. He cleaned up the bathroom and thoroughly inspected it for telltale

signs. Then, while consulting his photo, he put her talc jar back on her dressing table precisely where it had been. He was back on the sofa beginning another nap by 10 o'clock.

Mickey was so excited that night wondering what would happen in the morning that he hardly slept. When the alarm clock rang, he stayed in bed until Elizabeth got up, knowing that if they arose at the same time, the coffee would be ready as Elizabeth finished showering. He placed her coffee on the dressing table and he read the newspaper to her, but when the decisive moment arrived, he was too nervous to watch. He raised the newspaper an inch or two to hide his eyes while Elizabeth dusted the garlic onto her chest. He listened intently behind the paper but heard nothing out of the ordinary. He lowered the newspaper and peered over the top. She was placing the powder puff back in its jar.

At precisely 8 o'clock, Elizabeth opened the front door, nodded a prim goodbye to Mickey, and said, as she always did, "I'll be home at the usual time." Mickey closed the front door behind her, did a little dance, and pumped his fist silently into the air.

The cow was on the roof.

IGNITION

"You *did* bring the medicine home, Arthur, didn't you?" The question, one part hope, three parts rebuke, hung in the oak-paneled vestibule like a neon sign as Arthur sloughed off his damp shoes to avoid soiling Adriana's carpet.

Homecoming, he thought, a concept in decline since those crisp football weekends in New Hampshire so long ago. His most vivid memory of those days was the thrill of looking into those green eyes as she stepped off the train from Boston. They still bewitched him. They still could put his ambitions at bay – temporarily – but at some point without his awareness, the excitement had faded. The marching band had stolen away.

"Oh, no! I'll run down to the drug store right now. Be back in a jiffy," he said slipping on his already clammy shoes.

Bells on the Christmas wreath jingled as he pulled the heavy inner door shut. Seconds later the storm door pulled itself shut, a clattery aluminum cymbal. Adriana had spent the last two nights sitting next to the crib listening to the crackly expirations of her baby and an occasional creak of their fine, old house as it braced against the winter wind. Finally they took their baby to the doctor. "Bronchitis. Not dangerous," she said in her shorthand speech. "Antibiotic for ten days, plenty of fluids, should be fine." She made staccato slashes on her prescription pad, ripped a page off,

smiled antiseptically, and exited quickly like a ballerina *jette'ing* off stage.

"Damn her," Adriana had said under her breath. "I'm not coming back here, ever! She hardly looked at Little Lou...treated him like a flat tire!" Arthur had felt this pique lately and thought how out of character it was. Despite the Italian theater that had played out daily in the Rosi home, Adriana was not a drama queen. "She never resorted to tantrums and tears to get her way when she was growing up," her oldest brother Franco had told Arthur once. "All she had to do was turn those green eyes on some guy and as often as not he would turn to putty."

In fact, Arthur had 'turned to putty' the first time he met Adriana. It happened late one afternoon as he was walking to the bus stop along an ancient sidewalk, cracked and crumpled by a hundred Boston winters. In the fading light he had kept his eyes on the uneven surface directly in front of him. But, as Fate would have it, he looked up in time to see her approaching. With each light, high-heeled step she took, his legs felt weaker. Her green eyes met his and he thought irrationally, 'She likes me.' She smiled at him, amused, but as he started to return her greeting, his toe hit a crack, and he pitched forward, banging his forehead on the sidewalk. It made him woozy briefly, but even when he had recovered his senses, he felt as if he were dreaming. He had managed to attract the attention of this beautiful woman, who was by then kneeling over him, and to have the presence of mind to say while still lying on the sidewalk, "I fell for you the moment I saw you." Adriana caught the quip and replied, "That's a pretty good

crack." Given this second chance, Arthur managed to return her smile, but he missed his bus.

They fell in love quickly despite coming from very different backgrounds. Adriana was the baby girl in a big, close Rosi family; Arthur, an only, lonely child. He saw her as naïve about life's hard realities because from his perspective she had never experienced adversity. As he saw it, her life had rolled out before her wrinkle-free: her parents fawned over her; her three older brothers protected her; she had suffered no losses, few slights, and only an occasional lonely Saturday night. "She probably didn't even have acne," he once said to his mother. By comparison, Arthur had had to contend with his parents' indifference towards him for as long as he could remember. He knew he was still paying the price for his troubled adolescence while Adriana's had been delivered to her 'tax free.' Arthur resented this and although he knew it was only one of life's inequities, he could not shake it.

Nor could he get past the thought that Adriana's easy passage through her early years would set her up for disappointments in later life. Those enchanting eyes may have dispelled trouble and contributed tranquility to her youth, but inevitably there would be con artists like him who would look past the beauty in those eyes and see vulnerabilities. Looking out his bedroom window one morning at the woods on the Rosi estate, he imagined her as a deer, serene and delicate, but more susceptible to the hunter than most because she could not sense his proximity. He wondered if she would always have

difficulty detecting life's scams and dangers because she so lacked cunning herself.

And yet, recently, he had begun to see signs that she was becoming more perceptive and more protective of her infant son. The day after taking Lou to the pediatrician, for example, Arthur overheard her talking to the doctor early in the morning. "I was very disappointed in the way you treated my baby yesterday, Doctor," she said scowling at the wall. "He's a person, you know. You treated him like a thing." She paused; the doctor had probably interrupted her. "How? I'll tell you how. You didn't greet him, show him any affection, or even smile at him. I'll bring him back once more, but if I don't see a change, you lose Louie as a patient. Thank you for your time," she added as an afterthought. She hung up abruptly. Arthur was stunned – and proud of her – and he made a note to tread lightly.

That night Arthur told her how impressed he was with the way she stuck up for Little Lou. "Well, her attitude makes me furious, Arthur! And you too, my goodness," she continued, "how could you forget to pick up the medicine? Where has your mind been lately?"

Arthur *had* felt distracted lately. He had not been able to concentrate or sleep well. As his work persona deteriorated, his standing atop the sales board fell. He had wrestled for years with feelings of insecurity, but had never sought professional help or even the shoulder of a confidante. He barely even acknowledged their existence. But this season they seemed to be thriving, drawing strength from the deep December cold.

He was thinking of himself, as was often the case, when he pulled into the pharmacy parking lot. He stepped

judiciously on patches of pavement between slush and sheet ice in an effort to preserve his Bally loafers. Like a puppet he made his way toward the building with jerky movements and unbalanced steps, Ichabod Crane in a cashmere overcoat. He pulled open the drug store door, sucking frigid air into the fluorescent glare and headed down an aisle of beauty aids and feminine hygiene supplies directly to the prescription pick-up window. "Merry Christmas, Sayuri," he said, "I'd like to pick up my son's prescription, *dozo*." He gave the Japanese word a saucy inflection. "Are you staying warm this frigid evening?"

Peering over the tops of her cheaters, her exotic eyes held his an instant too long. "I am warm," she said in unaccented English. Her smile crossed toward him in slow motion. "And you?" She turned to retrieve his package, and added over the graceful curve of her shoulder, "You need to learn more than *dozo*, Arthur. 'Please' is not enough."

"And you are too much," he countered. "When do my lessons start?" he asked handing her his credit card.

"Whenever you think you are ready."

"I was born ready, my dear."

The transaction was far too quick but not exactly painless, Arthur thought, although Sayuri's coy repartee and willowy movements did lift his spirits. He thought about her on the drive home. His gift for listening and knowing intuitively what to say would work on her. It always worked, professionally and socially. It made him money. He was imagining a trip to Kyoto with her for the

holidays as he entered the vestibule again and removed his coat and wet shoes.

"You have the medicine *this* time, I hope."

~~~

Arthur clenched his jaw, closed his eyes, and bent over, hands on knees, as if he had just run a 200-meter sprint. There he remained for a few seconds, staring at his damp socks. The car key dug into his knee. He stood and ran his thumb along its pointed teeth and smooth grooves, thinking. "I've got it, Hon," he called back cheerfully, but he slipped the key into his pocket rather than hanging it on its hook in the hall.

After giving the baby his antibiotic, Adriana heated the minestrone she had made and put up last fall. Her mother considered minestrone with its earthy nutrition and aroma the remedy for all life's ills. "It'll do you good," she would say. So Adriana bustled, grating Parmesan to sprinkle on the soup and drizzling lemon-flavored olive oil on thick slices of sourdough. When Arthur appeared from the bedroom wearing a cardigan she had given him, she smiled and Arthur sensed the grating effects of the doctor's appointment were wearing off. He put on Christmas music and they sipped a Chateau Margaux.

"You look like a content and beautiful and slightly tired mom," he said. "Here's to you and Little Lou and his quick recovery." The toast worked. This precise stroke freed him from the doghouse and her from the doldrums. Its genius lay not in the mention of her maternity, or beauty, or worry over her baby's health, but in the acknowledgment of her weariness. That counterintuitive ingredient converted what might have been heard as an

empty compliment into insightful honesty and appreciation. Arthur knew the words would work even as they spilled casually from his mouth. Adriana's eyes stroked him as she raised her glass and rubbed his stocking feet with hers. They packed that night, mostly in silence, for a three-night visit with her parents.

~~~

For Arthur, visiting the Rosi family was like being in the chorus of a five-act Italian opera. The stage was the vast, white, mirrored living room of Adriana's grandfather. Papa Lou, the family's ninety-some-year-old patriarch, had landed in America almost eighty years ago, alone except for a small roll of worthless *lire* notes his family had struggled to save for his start in the new country. He had chanced upon work in a butcher shop where he was paid in fatty scraps and drinking water, but shrewd and alert as a jackal, he had snapped at an improbable opportunity and built a fortune in the dog food industry.

He had married and sired five children. As they grew, he had demonstrated, demanded, and rewarded loyalty to the family above all else, the Sicilian way, and he paid big money, as endowments when necessary, to get all his children and grandchildren, boys and girls, the best American educations he could. Each Christmas he presided in midnight blue serge and spanking white shirt, buttoned at the neck but without tie, over his forty-four over-fed, tightly knit, well-tailored and bejeweled progeny and their spouses. The flamboyant Rosi Christmas was more a celebration of family, their religion, than a Christian holiday.

They celebrated Adriana especially, Arthur thought. She had special status. She was their princess, adored and coddled, and when she produced Little Lou her stature grew. Motherhood was an absolute by the family's standards, far more regal than plain matrimony. The family celebrated Little Lou's arrival as if Adriana and Arthur had saved the family from extinction. They showered him with silver spoons and mugs, certificates of deposit for his education, plastic mobiles that played xylophone music, and mountains of designer clothes, including infant sports jerseys emblazoned with numbers on their tiny sleeves and 'Little Lou' arcing across their narrow backs.

Arthur was recognized too. On the baby's first visit 'home' Papa Lou embraced Arthur for the first time. The shriveled jackal, regnant but warm, had reached his mottled hands up, up to Arthur's face, pulled him forward as in a bow, and kissed him on both cheeks. *Bene, bene, Arturo*, he said, *benvenuto*. This benediction brought tears to Arthur's eyes and a change to his standing in the family. He had been accepted as Adriana's husband and enjoyed for his charm, but after the *abraccio* he belonged. He was then an ordained son and a beneficiary of their code. Business opportunities and contacts materialized, invitations arrived from names known only to Adriana, family members called him at the office simply for morale checks, a standard Rosi practice.

The authenticity of the family's embrace touched Arthur so deeply he could not discuss it with Adriana – it would have swamped his emotions – but it also frightened him. He feared that like water it would soak its way down

to the bottom of his façade, through all the crevices, and make a mess. He had made a success by staying on the surface, where he could breathe, and by keeping others there. He was a master of the initial impression, an art form that only appeared to have depth, and his business acumen was a gift actually sharpened by his remove from humanity. His detachment made him less vulnerable to an artful analyst's pitch, more clinical and shrewd in his judgments. His response to the Rosis' affection had to be contrived, he thought, because that's what he was. It also had to be discovered. In a family so genuinely devoted to one another, whether he spent time with them or avoided them, eventually they would see through him. They would know he did not fit.

Yet, Arthur knew a good deal when he saw one. He knew beyond a doubt that the Rosi deal was the best one he would ever see. The moment the Jackal's spindling fingers had touched his cheeks and pulled him in he knew he had an opportunity to belong. Inclusion, the need he had denied for years, hung before him within reach. And yet a family's embrace was only an apparition to Arthur, an ethereal reflection in the distance.

His own father had been locked down tighter than his little Texas savings and loan company at night. Guards inside and out. On the rare occasions when they actually conversed, Arthur was amazed at how fast his father's opinions formed and hardened. They seemed to crystallize instantly in the chill of his pronouncements and rain down upon Arthur in jagged pieces. His father deserted the family during Arthur's sophomore year in college,

disappeared without a word of farewell, without a trace, but with a tidy sum from his S&L.

Communication with his mother was not much better because her primary interest was business, not Arthur. She sold real estate, owned a 'U Frame It' shop, and co-owned the Dairy Queen franchise in town. "Come work in the frame shop, Honey," she said repeatedly when Arthur was in high school. Arthur would heave a heavy sigh and say, "I'd rather light myself on fire every night at the State Fair, Mom."

"It's a cash cow, Artie," she would reply undeterred. "It could be yours one day if you'd just learn the business." She loved Arthur, but not so much as she loved competition in the market place, and she was sweet to him, but he always knew when she was with him her mind was elsewhere. When her husband disappeared, she sold her assets and went to live with her sister in Austin where she opened a boutique. Arthur usually received a card from her on his birthday.

Life with these parents was lonely and painful for Arthur. As a youngster, numbness settled over his tender psyche. This provided him with some protection from the sting of his father's intransigence and the disappointment of his mother's lack of interest. As he grew older, he learned to hide his disappointments and his feelings from them – and from everyone. He found life easier that way. Then, like the miniscule tracings of a seismograph long before an earthquake, an awareness of his parents' vulnerabilities began to register on his young brain.

The epiphany occurred during the summer he turned fifteen and won the state spelling bee. Even though his

parents had given him no encouragement during the endless hours he studied for it, his mother crowed loudly after he won, and his father strutted around town as if he had been having an affair with Miss Texas. How stupid, Arthur thought, seething in bed one hot night. *My* accomplishment inflates *their* egos. Then the revelation: instead of resenting their false pride, he realized he could have taken advantage of it. If only I had seen this coming, he thought, I could have finagled some money out of it or a car or something. He should have known. That summer 'Think Like Your Enemy' became his motto and neither his parents nor anyone else would get off free again.

In September Arthur found himself sitting behind Marilyn Connery in algebra class. He daydreamed about her as he watched her index finger twirl strands of her lovely hair. Occasionally a twist would expose the soft skin of her neck. What does she need? Arthur thought. What is she thinking?

"Artie," she asked one day pointing at the board, "is that a plus or minus after the 'x' in the first problem?" Then later, "Artie, can you see what he wrote at the end of the last line?" Walking to the lunchroom after class he asked, "Do you think you need glasses?"

"Yeah, for sure," she said, "but they'd make me look dorky." Arthur sympathized. He listened and encouraged her to visit an optometrist. When she made an appointment, he accompanied her and told her the frames made her look sophisticated and older. "Maybe you'll be able to buy beer now," he suggested. By homecoming he had won; he had kissed that lovely neck.

Sometimes he worked acquaintances just for practice. By the end of his sophomore year in college several bartenders considered Arthur a close friend and let him drink for free. He sharpened his skills on professors, learning to decorate his false empathy for their courses with the academic phrases they used. A Professor Bond, who taught deviant psychology, became so infatuated with Arthur he suggested they spend a weekend in Niagara Falls, thus contributing another maxim to Arthur's growing stock: well-planned ploys can produce unexpected results. By the time he earned his MBA and landed his first job, Arthur had fine-tuned his scheme. First, at every meeting, he would subtly encourage his clients to talk about themselves. Immediately thereafter, he would jot down every detail he could remember – pets' names, grandparents' alma maters, a wife's dress size, the names of friends and acquaintances, etc. Nothing was insignificant. He also recorded his impressions of his clients and their ambitions and he always perused a client's dossier before talking to him whether in person or on the phone. His clients soon came to believe Arthur had an uncanny memory which helped account for the extraordinary success he had in persuading one client after another to accept his investment recommendations. Arthur was careful not to mention his system to others in his office. He did not intend to share it.

Some of his clients did make money, of course, and Arthur earned – in addition to his substantial commissions – their future business and admiration. But their opinions of him mattered little; they were only marks to him. He reflected on this unflattering reality before

sunup one morning while feeding Little Lou. Everyone in my life is a mark, he thought. Even as his tiny son sucked and gurgled in his arms, he contemplated how beneficial the little guy's arrival had been to his standing in the family, how clever he had been to name him after the family patriarch. Jesus, Arthur thought! How cold I am! Just like my old man. Locked away all alone surrounded by my wife and son and Adriana's whole, goddamned, beautiful family!

Light edged into the sky that morning, fading black to rumpled grays. A crenellated skyline appeared mystically under the clouds. To Arthur's sleepy, introspective mind, the notched design loomed as a distant fortress, challenging his intentions, protecting the past. No, he thought, I will overcome him. Screw *him*! He lifted Little Lou to his shoulder, a warm, soft bun. They touched, whiskers and wisps. Arthur lay his hand on the pink velvet back and thumped expertly between the shoulder blades. I *will* make this work, he promised himself, as he admired his attractive face in the mirror.

~~~

Arthur went to the office the next day, but Christmas carols, rum eggnog, and holiday familiarity overcame his to-do list. Participation was politic, so he put on a Santa Claus hat and schmoozed. He discreetly gave his secretary her gift. "Open it tomorrow," he urged her, "so it can be part of your Christmas day." She hugged him, hesitated for a beat, then planted an alcoholic kiss on the side of his mouth.

Arthur was home by four. The frigid air seemed to congeal and push against him as he shuttled between the

warm house and the frozen driveway hauling stuff and loading the BMW. A twenty-pound spiral-cut ham, a collapsible crib, the bassinet, anchored securely behind the front passenger seat, suitcases, yoga mat, a jumbo-size wheel of cheese, two hi-tech pillows for Adriana's neck and back, an ab strengthening apparatus, infinite gifts, even an orchid, carefully protected and immobilized in the car's pre-warmed interior. He utilized space like a NASA engineer until only the driver's seat and a space for Adriana behind it were free.

The fateful migration began after dark. Adriana, cradling Little Lou, who was bundled beyond sight against the cold, descended the slippery outdoor stairs and inched her way toward the car. Arthur hovered, an arm around her waist, and fussed as she ducked into the back seat and tucked Lou into the bassinet. Arthur's icy toes throbbed as he slid into the warm interior and his frigid fingers could barely grasp the ignition key. It fell and as he leaned forward to retrieve it his nose released two remarkable streams of phlegm. They dangled over his leg like shiny bungee cords. Shit, he thought, sniffing mightily and glancing at Adriana in the rearview mirror as the wet cords ascended and stuck to his lip. He was embarrassed and angry, but Adriana, seated behind him, did not see this. He wiped the mess with the back of his glove.

"Off we go," he said into the mirror, disguising his darkening mood.

"Can we have some Christmas music instead of that depressing political news?" the voice behind him asked.

Halfway down the block Arthur could not remember packing his briefcase. Shit, he thought again, and pulled to the curb to think.

"What now, Hon?" The detached voice landed in mid-thought.

"Shhhh. I'm trying to remember something."

"Remember what? Can't you try to remember *while* you're driving?"

He returned to the house without answering. He remembered putting it down at the front door as they left. It was not in sight as he bounded up the stairs. Ah, there it was between the storm door and the main door. Must have put it down while locking up. What's wrong with me? he thought. I hate this cold.

Silence fell as they drove away again, the muffled crunch of snow beneath their tires. They drove past heavily blanketed lawns and boughs and stoops, through window-high tunnels of crumpled snow banks, and by the honey-glow warmth spilling from neighbors' windows into the black night. The town was festooned with Xmas lights and décor. An eight-foot, inflatable snowman bobbed and weaved in the wind in front of the Shell station as they turned onto the turnpike.

"Arthur, are you all right? You seem kind of not yourself lately, kind of scattered, you know?"

"Yeah, I'm fine. I'm looking forward to seeing your family."

"Really? Well, I've been worried about you lately. You're always so organized, so in control, you know? You make your neat lists and cross things off. It's not like you

to forget things, especially important things like medicine and your briefcase." After a pause she said, "I love you, A."

"I know," Arthur whispered, but having just been rebuked he could not bring himself to say 'I love you too.' Her so-called worry about him sounded more like criticism and her growing dependence on him was suffocating. "Don't worry, A," he said as if all were well. "I'm okay, really. I was just thinking this morning as the sun came up how much Lou means to me. I *am* going to make this work."

It was an uncharacteristic slip of the tongue, and he feared even as the words were escaping from his lips that the remark could do serious damage. He never spoke extemporaneously. He always calculated the effect of his words before uttering them. What *was* wrong with him?

The slip heightened his senses. He was aware of the harsh silence between him and Adriana, of her rapid breathing, of Gene goddamned Autry on the radio. He felt the heater's oppressive warmth and took in the foul scents of leather upholstery, baby powder, and cheese. He caught a glimpse of Adriana in the rearview mirror, her hand over her mouth as if to muffle a sound. Their eyes met for an instant – before Adriana looked away – but in that split second Arthur saw surprise and confusion. It made him feel guilty. He doubted that she would step up and ask directly, "What did you mean by that remark, Arthur?" Or, "Does that mean you think our marriage is failing?" That was not her style; she was not brave. But fear can produce unlikely results so he seized the initiative and began to talk.

"What I mean," he said striving to find the same pitch and tone as the slip, "is that I've decided to give every ounce of energy I have to my family – like Papa Lou did. I made that promise to myself this morning while I was holding Little Lou and watching the sunrise. It was kind of an epiphany."

Some time passed before Adriana replied and when she did her voice sounded high and tight. Arthur tried to observe her in the mirror again, but she kept her head turned so he could see neither her face nor her eyes. First, she spoke some baby talk to Little Lou. She was probably playing for time, uncertain about what to say, how to act. Arthur knew what she was thinking: My husband is behaving strangely; Is my baby safe? What should I do? When she finally spoke she said only, "I couldn't hear you."

"I said 'I love you too' and I'm going to do everything to make sure you guys are always happy." As his words fell on her ears, Arthur was aware of how hypocritical they must have sounded next to the authenticity of his slip. He was certain she had heard it.

With his words ricocheting in his head and a lump in his throat the size of a walnut, Arthur set the cruise control at 65. Adriana put her hand on her baby's hand, closed her eyes, and pretended to sleep. The 90 endless miles to the Rosi home began to fall away in the darkness behind them.

~~~

Arthur's instinct was to talk his way out of any hole. He assumed this one was deepening with each minute Adriana spent ruminating on his remark. Little Lou was solid common ground, an obvious starting point, so he

turned his head toward the back seat and asked, "How was Little Lou's cold today, A?" There was no answer. He knew she was not asleep but he could not see her because she was seated directly behind him. So, he turned his head again and called her name a little louder. "Adriana?"

"I'm trying to rest. I worked today, you know."

"Aw, come on. Talk to me awhile. It'll help keep me awake," Arthur said cheerfully.

"You need *help*," Adriana shot back angrily.

A dagger of an accusation! The woman who was so docile, who had never laid blame on anyone – other than the doctor recently – had just laid the wood on him. He did *not* need help! What a crock! He wanted to reply, but was so taken aback by her aggressiveness he said nothing.

Adriana, huddled in the back seat, was so upset she was shaking. If Arthur had been able to see her, he would have been touched and might have offered her his hand as comfort. Such contact, however brief, might have persuaded him that Adriana's words had escaped her lips before she knew what she was saying, just as his dreadful slip had. They had common ground, reasons to be understanding, but forgiveness requires human warmth to grow in the face of adversity; and Adriana, curled up in her blanket behind Arthur, was out of sight and out of reach.

So, at that moment, in Arthur's mind, she personified her brazen and insulting words: 'You need help.' He had kicked himself often for treating Adriana poorly, but this time he felt legitimately aggrieved. He had worked that day too and loaded the car and put up with Adriana's changing moods for months. In their four years of

marriage they had never truly hurt each other with words, but this was different.

Nonetheless, Arthur was a calculator; he did not shoot from the hip. He appreciated how much being married to Adriana contributed to his life and his lifestyle. Without the many wealthy investors her family sent him, his income and reputation would look different. So, he tried again to talk to her civilly. "Adriana," he said, turning toward the backseat, "I've got to pee and get some gas. What's the exit we usually take for our break?" There was no answer.

He was about to repeat himself in a louder voice when Adriana said, "I don't want to stop now. I want to get home as soon as possible."

"Maybe you didn't hear me. My bladder's full. I've gotta stop. What's the exit number?"

"Don't stop now. We're only 30 minutes from home." The Princess knew precisely where they were. She had not been asleep, and now she had spoken. She really had her back up, Arthur noted. She just wanted to be home with her protective Daddy and brothers. Her stubborn attitude, toward one of his basic bodily functions no less, was new. Normally she would end a disagreement by saying 'suit yourself', followed by a sigh, and the cold shoulder, but she had hardened. As he was debating what to do, a sign appeared overhead that said, 'Service Area 1 Mile.' The die was cast.

~ ~ ~

Without another word, Arthur pulled into the service area. He slid out of the car at the pump and was blown sideways by a bitterly cold wind. A teenager wearing a

thick watch cap pulled down over his eyebrows and ears and a greasy Patriots warm-up jacket shambled up. "How mucha want?" he asked.

"Fill 'er up," Arthur said. "Won't take too much."

Arthur headed rapidly for the gas station wondering how the kid got stuck with the Christmas Eve shift. He went to the bathroom, bought a packet of peanut butter crackers, and was on his way out as the kid shuffled through the door. "Be $15.50, man."

Arthur handed him $40. "Keep the change, young man, and keep warm," he said over his shoulder as he jogged to the car, head down, shoulders hunched, hands jammed into his pockets. He slipped into the warm interior as quickly and quietly as possible and immediately dialed the heater to 'high.' "Goddamn it's cold," he said to himself as he accelerated onto the turnpike.

Snow began to fall. Lucent flurries seemed to funnel toward the car from ninety degrees of darkness. They flew, a storm of mini-meteorites, inexorably inbound, spellbinding, racing to a focal point in front of Arthur. There they converged and vanished in silence. I am entering the vortex for all light he mused, munching on a peanut butter cracker. I am flying into the core of darkness. Captain Kirk, deactivate the light magnetron, he commanded telepathically, but the flakes continued to beam in on him, relentlessly, hypnotically, and the BMW continued to bore through them, hurling them into cold chaos in its wake.

He flicked his beams from high to low to narrow the scope of the mesmerizing display on his windscreen and told himself to concentrate. How devastating will that

stupid slip be to Adriana, he wondered? She's not as fragile as she sounds. It probably made her think I'm ready to jump ship like my old man. That wouldn't be such a big loss to her, really. Her big, tight family and all their money, they'd swaddle her in sympathy. She'd recover, no doubt about it. This thought gave Arthur some solace. He realized he was not inexorably bound to his present life.

'I *am* going to make this work.' He pondered the comment again. God, one slip. It's like cracking a keystone.

Bing Crosby crooned in the console.

May your days be merry and bright,
And may all your Christmases be white ...

The velvet baritone carried him back to Texas. God, how Mom loved der Bingle, he recalled. *She* wasn't as fragile as she seemed either. Arthur pondered his mother's remarkable rejuvenation and popped his last peanut butter cracker. Once she dug her way out of the rubble of her marriage, she must have felt so free, he thought. Absolutely liberated! Arthur smiled to himself. Always the businessperson, she had purchased a nondescript boutique in Austin. As the city had grown, her shop had grown and prospered, she wrote on her annual Christmas card. Arthur could imagine: It had consumed her energy and given her friends and independence. It returned her soul to her, he mused.

But I can do better he told himself. Survival is the bottom rung. I also want to find some fun in life. Sayuri. Now that would be fun. His musings had delivered her to

him several times during the last twenty-four hours. He recalled their conversation the night before and wondered where she thought it had been leading. She is gorgeous, he thought. Beautiful eyes, willowy figure, must be smart too to be a pharmacist, but she has a risqué redneck quality too. Sexy combination – Japanese hillbilly.

An exit sign shot by on Arthur's right and startled him back to the moment. "Adriana. Sorry to wake you, but we take Exit 14 to your parents' house, right?" he said. There was no answer from the seat behind him. He had been so deep in thought he had forgotten about their feud.

"Adriana? Not too far now. Gotta wake up," he said. There was no sound of movement. Arthur turned toward the back seat and gasped. The bassinet was gone!

"Adriana!" the shrillness in his voice sliced into the silence. He craned his neck harder to look directly behind him. She was not there either. Oh, my God!

The car slowed as Arthur's mind raced, spinning without traction for a moment, then grabbing hold. The gas station, he thought. It had to be. She must've jumped out there ... while he was in the bathroom ... to change Lou, to leave him...Holy shit!

Several miles ahead, consumed with impatience, he finally was able to exit the turnpike, cross over it to an entrance, and head back. By then he had driven fifteen minutes or so, maybe less, he hoped. Adriana's going to think I've lost my mind. Or, maybe she'll think I'd had enough and left her at a gas station on the turnpike on a cold, dark Christmas Eve. If she could think that, I could do it. But this could happen to anyone, couldn't it? Probably has happened to others ... lots of times.

The flakes flew at him, heavier now, and with greater precision the faster he drove. A reverse radiation. A million relentless obligations converging on him. Curious, he thought, they target me whether I'm running away or returning, coming or going. It's unnatural. Direction, orientation, intention – they have no bearing – I keep getting hammered.

Or maybe this hasn't happened to others, he thought. His conscience was insisting he be honest. Accidents don't just happen. I wonder if Adriana's called her dad yet. She's probably told her family I've left her, that I'm not fit for this. Who knows? What do *I* know anyway? I can make money. I know that. I can provide stuff: nice house, clothes. Look at this damn car after all! Doctor bills paid. Hatred ain't such a bad teacher really, is it? He was rolling now, over 80 mph, thoughts and doubts stormed inside, matching the frenzy without.

I really do want to make this work, he insisted. Don't I? The Rosi family is like a big comforter to me. I could get under it. I could warm up – probably. They'll take me as if I were their real son this Christmas. Arthur could imagine Papa Lou calling him *figlio mio* in his ancient, hoarse voice and Adriana's brothers rolling on the white carpet with Little Lou laughing.

Little Lou, that tiny, warm bun. He was at the crux of it all really. Arthur always knew he was. "What's best for him" Arthur heard himself asking aloud. "Me?" Like father like son, he thought. Gotta be some truth in that. If I'd never known my own damn father I'd be way better off, he thought. Then I'd have only his genes and I wouldn't be so goddamned angry at him – and everybody. Then I'd be

less inclined to cut and run. He stifled a sound. I could've handled only the genes.

The Mormon Tabernacle Choir rejoiced.

Oh little town of Bethlehem
How still we see thee lie
Above thy deep and dreamless sleep,
The silent stars go by.

The carol in the background calmed Arthur and the storm receded temporarily into the night, allowing him a moment to think. He had a choice: take the next exit and return to his family, or head to Boston and a new life. A moment of truth. "They do not come along often," he thought, "so I must be true to myself." With this realization, an imperceptible sigh of relief slipped from deep within him. He knew there was only one answer for him. At that instant, a green and white informational sign came into view:

Service Area Exit 1 Mile.
Boston 46 miles.

THE ELEPHANT HUNT

could feel that familiar tug and knew Marion was calling me to him. He was in Buffalo, a dark destination shivering up there on the lake in the grip of late autumn, but I knew I would go to him even though I was not sure he would know me when I arrived.

Dear Marion, he had been gone three years from my life but never a day from my heart. Time and toil allow me to admit that now, to myself if not to others, but the years had taken their toll. They had tinkered with my memory of him, made him into a human kaleidoscope who changed with each reflection. He was still both alluring and perplexing, as he was the night I followed him through a reception line in an elegant Georgetown home. After introducing himself to the hostess, he gestured toward me and said in the sonorous, radio announcer voice he affected occasionally, "Mrs. Worthington, may I introduce Captain Frank Grimm of the Detroit Home for the Tall." There I stood, my height lending credibility to the introduction, but stymied because I didn't have the wit or moxie to summon up an impersonation of Captain Grimm. Mrs. Worthington, her social instincts on high alert, let me off the hook. She raised an eyebrow, extended a limp hand, and said in a semi-British accent, "You are most

welcome, Captain." As I wandered among the guests, I realized that if I had introduced Marion that way, he would have conjured up a memorable Captain Grimm with an odd background to explain how a person of his average stature had landed at the Home for the Tall and he would have enchanted Mrs. Worthington. I would love to have heard his Grimm tale, but it would have made me feel unimaginative and not quite sure who Marion was.

~~~

We met by chance at a Holiday Inn bar during a deaf persons bowling league banquet. At the far end of the room the league champs, wearing chartreuse team shirts with nicknames stitched in cursive over the pockets, were gathering at a u-shaped table laden with trophies and certificates. They were hoisting frosty mugs, signing with abandon, and posing for group pictures, arms around each other, but the room was eerily quiet.

Marion was perched on a stool, his back to the bar, observing the camaraderie. When I sat down next to him he said, "Deaf bowlers partying hard." I must have looked at him quizzically because he gestured with his head at the raucous silence emanating from the other end of the room. I still didn't get it. What's up with this guy, I thought? He didn't look drunk. His blue eyes were clear and inquisitive. They were wide-set in a cherub-like face, pudgy and fair. Their gaze hinted at innocence, and yet I sensed it was a false innocence, worn like stage paint for effect. His smile was theatrical too. It came on too quickly and looked overly sincere.

I felt edgy engaging an unknown male in conversation in a bar. I was young and inexperienced at sending and

receiving signals. So I did what I still do: I tried to project a neutral image and observe discriminately. What I saw was a man with panache, but it was not natural; it was under construction. His modish haircut suggested a stylist, not a barber. He wore expensive, tasseled loafers without socks, a look I had not seen before, and jewelry, a heavy copper bracelet and a tiny gold earring that was not readily visible under his longish dark hair. He emitted an aftershave scent, pine I think, and a meticulously casual look, which was at odds with his girth: his polo shirt stretched over sizeable love handles and billowing biceps; his madras Bermuda shorts strained at the seams.

"You just gotta admire 'em," he said. Then, after a pause, as if we had come in together, "Be right back. Order us a couple of beers...on me." He walked down to the party and spoke to one of the bowlers. I watched with admiration knowing that whatever he was doing I could never do. It was too nervy. A minute later the man shook Marion's hand, waved like a semaphore signaler for attention, and signed something to the group. It produced laughter and applause and Marion bowed modestly.

"What was that about?" I asked when he sat down again on his stool.

"Oh, nothing. I just told them 'Square Earl' Anthony would be proud of them, that the next round was on me...and I asked them to please keep the noise down."

"Square Earl Anthony?" I was beginning to feel a little disconnected.

"You've never heard of Square Earl? Guess he's not a household name. He's the Babe Ruth of bowling. Cheers," he said, raising his beer and introducing himself.

During the years I knew Marion, I never knew him to go bowling. I don't even recall his mentioning bowling again. He had little interest in sports, but he did have the damnedest assortment of information in his head and he used it to maximum effect.

We talked for a while, exchanged phone numbers, and walked out to the parking lot together. He stopped at a bilious green Nash Rambler. "This is Anthrax," he said. "Puts out more toxins than Con-Edison and a herd of farting elephants." What can you say to a remark like that? Almost anything will sound flat and stupid, but I did chuckle and I thought about him on the way home.

~~~

Three days later Marion phoned. I was delighted. He lived nearby and we began to spend time together. He was unusually thoughtful and offered to baby-sit my cat while I was on a business trip. Not many guys would do that. While traveling I fancied ways to initiate conversations with him that would lead to our opening up to one another. I refined and rehearsed them like a perfectionist playwright, but when I got home, I choked. I didn't dare offer up any of my carefully crafted gambits. Not yet, I thought. Maybe he'd be insulted.

Instead, we discussed my cat. What a comedown, although he did look different since my return. His fur stuck out as if he were perpetually in attack mode. "What's the deal with Atticus?" I asked. "He looks like he was electrocuted."

"Well, he looked kind of dirty and unkempt so I gave him a beauty treatment," Marion said. I admit Atticus had an untidy look. He spent hours in his lair under the house

hunting insects in the cobwebs. "I bought him a peach-lilac-aloe shampoo/conditioner product recommended by Hollywood starlets," Marion continued. "Took him right in the shower with me. That didn't work out so well the first time. You remember the famous painting *Tiger's Revenge* by Claude Balls? That's me, Kelly," he said with a wink. "Clawed balls and everything else. My body looked like I play goalie for the local dart team. So, next time we went in I wore my rubber raincoat and gardening gloves. Gave him a shampoo and a trim afterwards. Blow-dried him – on low, of course – and I think he feels better. Really do. I'm giving *you* one next," he teased.

Atticus didn't resent him. In fact, every time Marion came over Atticus would run at him full tilt and leap to his shoulder, purring on the fly. That's what Marion did. He stole the show. He gave so much I couldn't keep up. Every time he returned from a trip he brought me a present. Most men don't do that either. The gifts were often books with titles like *Diseases of Chinchilla* or *The Life of Myron Floren,* and they were always inscribed by the authors (in Marion's handwriting). Mr. Floren had written, "To my best friend, Kelly. Squeezing you is even better than squeezing my Pancordian. Forever, Myron."

This, along with the warm hugs he gave me when we hadn't seen each other for some time, gave me ample opportunity to respond. I loved him for this, but I held back, so I resented him too for making me aware of how timid I was. I was self-conscious because of the social stigma we had and I was so terrified by the threat of AIDS I would not have climbed into bed with anyone. Back then it was a deadly, mysterious, rampant disease. Marion was

braver than I. He seemed willing to be himself despite what people thought. So I lay awake at night kicking myself for being reluctant and distant and encouraging myself to share my thoughts with him. But it didn't happen. I worried about what my parents would think, especially my macho father, and I couldn't bear the scenes I imagined at home: the tears and harsh words that would scar. I felt handcuffed. I *was* handcuffed. So I did nothing.

~~~

All kinds of recollections caromed around in my head during that night drive to Buffalo. They boomed like thunder clouds warning of the storm ahead. But they also strengthened my resolve to apologize to Marion for not being open and honest with him.

I knew this would not be easy and Marion would not help. He was reticent too, truth be told. Despite all we went through together, the important stuff between us, the expressions of affection and concern for each other, was conveyed by inference or with humor. Marion had a knack for derailing serious discussion if it was about him. He did it when we first met back at the Holiday Inn. That afternoon just to make conversation I'd asked him where he worked.

"I'm with AGC."

"AGC?" I asked.

"Arthur Godfrey Collections," he explained. "It's a foundation that collects his memorabilia. I'm in charge of ukulele procurement. The pay is excellent, but my security clearance may not be renewed." As you can appreciate, this didn't lead to an in-depth discussion of Marion's career dreams, but in time I came to understand that

losing his clearance was Marion-speak for losing his job. He never said directly that he worked for some secretive organization, but he implied as much. In Washington when someone is reluctant to say where he works, everyone assumes he is a secret agent of some kind.

One day he walked in and after his usual embrace from Atticus said, "Well, I just took a job with Olivetti. Do you think I'll be able to sell office equipment?"

"Really?" I asked, astonished. I *had* to ask because sometimes I didn't know if he was serious. He nodded awkwardly. "What happened to the job with AGC?" which had become our code word for his real job.

"I really didn't fit in," he said, and that was code too. "Plus they were disappointed with my attendance record in French class." Marion had been studying French in preparation for an assignment to Morocco. He spoke German well and would have been an excellent language student because he was a world-class mimic, but he was also a night person. Class began at nine a.m., which was several hours out of sync with Marion's body clock.

"*Mais je parle très bien français* ..." he continued.

"That sounds pretty good to me."

"Ah oui, but eet eez basically bullsheet. *Il y a* some French words *mais efficacement* eet eez zhust zee French sound, *pas plus*. The teacher thought I was mocking her language but I wasn't. When she spoke to me weez zat aksont, I had to say somezing, *n'est-ce pas*? *Quel fromage*! It made her furious."

No doubt, Marion was out of sync. The unwritten policy then was 'don't ask, don't tolerate.' His originality did not meet AGC's button-down criteria. So they fired

him for being late to language class. He knew all along he was a misfit there – like "dog poopie in a punch bowl" was his expression – but he still felt deeply offended by the loss of that job and the discrimination. I tried to console him. I told him things would work out, but I should have done more. I should have put my arms around him and told him it was AGS's great loss, that he was better off without them, and that we were in this together. Instead, I watched as his life became a scavenger hunt for the right job, the right mate, indeed, even the right Marion.

~ ~ ~

That night on the way to Buffalo, *Ophelia,* a tune by The Band, came on the car radio and carried me back to the first crisis Marion and I faced together. Against my better judgment, I had begun seeing someone, a woman. Her name was Ophelia. She was an actress at a local repertoire theater, a hypochondriac, who claimed her Weimaraner was diabetic, and a magnet for society's estranged souls. During our year together we spent hours creating gourmet delights in her kitchen and talking about theater. She taught me much about cooking, but mostly she offered solace. And she drank. She poured a jigger of vodka into her morning OJ, brandy into her coffee. By the time she gave her dog Sweetness his 10 a.m. insulin shot, she was lit.

One night after dinner at which we had both had too much wine she wriggled right up on top of me on the sofa, put both my hands in hers, and said earnestly, "I have to tell you something."

"What?" I said. "Is it bad?"

"No, it's good." Then after biting her lip white and with all the tenderness an actress could bring to bear she said, "I think I love you."

"I love you too," I said recklessly and she took me to her bed that night. The next morning I was so ashamed. Romantic love had never entered my mind. Ophelia was a lonely, vulnerable friend whom I did not want to hurt. I knew I'd have to find a solution and it would not be easy.

So, of course, I turned to Marion. Our talks about the Ophelia Predicament – Marion called it the OP – offered me ideal opportunities to tell him how I felt about him. We had grown so close we communicated without talking and sensed each other's moods. We were in lockstep and it was wonderful to be so connected to another soul, but we had wandered into an impasse: we simply could *not* discuss the elephant in our lives. If Marion had raised it, I would have followed his lead, but he avoided it too. The elephant was growing and I knew eventually that we would have to acknowledge it or it would destroy us, but for the moment, I had what I wanted most: Marion and my health.

So, we talked about the OP instead. "You've tied a Gordian knot around your gonads," Marion summarized. "Think Houdini, bound in chains, hanging from his ankles, locked in a trunk, underwater – shit man, if he could escape, we can." He always said 'we,' he listened endlessly, and he shared his insights. They were sound and often shrewd and he let me know he was 100 percent on my side and that we would find our way out of my affair together. I needed that assurance more than anything as Ophelia and I hacked away at that knot and finally broke free.

Marion did me one better – he always did. He walked away from our elephant and into an engagement. Inga, his betrothed, was blond, muscular, rake-thin, and 6'2". Both her towering parents had played for Norwegian Olympic volleyball teams and the shortest of her three thin brothers was 6'6". A hilarious photo was taken of the family and Marion at a formal New Year's Eve party in Oslo. He said he looked like a 'gnome in mourning' standing, or was he squatting, in his tuxedo among those towering, gaunt figures. I laughed at that picture until my stomach hurt and I think it helped convince Marion and Inga to abandon their marriage plans: the wedding pictures would have been too great a burden.

Marion persisted, though, and converted his second fiancée, Angel, into his first wife. She was the daughter of a Rhode Island Mafioso kingpin – allegedly. The wedding must have cost $50,000 and is the only time I will wear a white tuxedo, unless the mob suggests it again. Angel was attractive enough, in a sequins-false-eyelashes-fishnet-stockings-style, but God only knows what Marion was thinking. *I* certainly didn't because he was uncomfortable discussing it and so was I. I was afraid that in my grief I'd say something impetuous and disappoint him. I knew *she* could never take him from me – we were simply too close to be split up by a woman – but I feared *I* could lose him with insinuating or insulting words and I didn't have the guts to risk that. So, I chose silence once again and the pain of living with it. To my great relief, but not to my surprise, the marriage lasted less than a year – even Marion couldn't play that role for long – and as his best friend I helped him find a good divorce lawyer. We were

both relieved to escape the gloved hand of the Mafia and, by default, to find ourselves together again.

Marion took an apartment near mine, but within six months he was gone. Our relationship had become stagnant, possibly because we had. Marion's job offered him no challenge or gratification. Our conversations were forced, we didn't laugh much, and I felt awkward when we were together. Frankly, it all hinged on our inability to enter into a physical relationship – or even discuss it. So, when Marion was offered an administrative job with the University of Buffalo, which included free tuition, he jumped at it. I took him out to dinner at his favorite restaurant his last night in town, but even then, facing possibly the end of our friendship, we did not mention our love for each other. I don't know why Marion stayed clear of this issue, but I know why I did: it was fear of AIDS. My calculation was simple: if he left, we would never have sex so my chances of getting AIDS would be zero. I was sacrificing a friendship to fear. I felt it was a cowardly and sensible thing to do. After dinner we went to my house for a nightcap. As the witching hour arrived, we looked at each other and fell into a long, wordless embrace in the kitchen. Then Marion turned and walked away. If we had gone to bed together that night, our story would have had a happier ending.

~~~

I was half way to Buffalo when I pulled off the interstate about three that morning for a coffee. 'Half Way to Buffalo': it sounded like a trucker's song Marion would like, or make up. He worked as a country-western DJ in college and would sometimes break out that singsong, DJ

voice he used with Mrs. Worthington. "Good morning, friends and neighbors. Ole Marion comin' right back at cha with another hour of the best in C Dubya to make your day slide by smoother'n spit on a brass door knob." Then he would fix you with his most insincere grin and those innocent baby blues and say, "This here music's good for moles, colds, and sore assholes; makes childbirth a pleasure."

My father liked country-western music too, and he thought the world of Marion. The first time they met my father took him in like a second son – without the baggage. I watched that chemistry every time we drove up for a weekend and it was unsettling. I had never felt close to my father. I thought he probably loved me, but he did keep his distance. Maybe he was ashamed of me because I didn't play sports and I liked to cook with my Mom. I was far from being a manly guy like him. I blamed him, of course – that's what teenagers do – for not understanding me, but I shouldn't have; even I didn't understand me then. Now I think we were both trying to figure me out. I was anxious and unhappy and he was quiet, very quiet around me.

Around Marion, though, he was almost outgoing – for an engineer. He worked for the Pennsylvania Department of Transportation in highway construction, not a profession that would have fascinated Marion – or anyone else for that matter. At Penn State he played linebacker for three years, which did impress some people. My father was pathologically analytical, economical with words, very fit, and socially out to lunch. (He wore his hard hat to my

parent-teacher meetings, for God's sake!) Who would have thought those two would hit it off so well?

My father was smart too. He read serious books, did crossword puzzles with a pen, played chess and he loved my Mom. He brought her flowers, never forgot her birthday, and seemed to understand her. He was perceptive. I imagine he understood the men on his highway crews too because sometimes at dinner he would analyze them for my mom in shrink-like depth and he clearly sympathized with them. The only time I saw him cry was at the funeral of a baby of one of his men. Marion was really touched by that and asked me if he had been a good father. I hedged my answer because I knew Marion admired him and I did not want to disappoint him by sounding too critical. So, I said I knew he loved me when I was little because he was the first parent into my school the day two gas boilers exploded and killed three kids. I told Marion he found me amongst all that wreckage. I told him of the moment I first saw him running toward me through the debris, rumbling like a bulldozer, ignoring the firemen who tried to stop him; he was snorting and red in the face. I had a nosebleed and couldn't hear well, but I felt safe as soon as I saw him, even before he touched me. He picked me up under one arm and ran past screaming people, damaged walls, through dust and acrid smells to the far edge of the playground where he put me down near a fire truck and looked me over carefully. Then he sat on the grass right behind me with his arms around me, breathing hard and shaking. We sat there together for a long time, as I remember it, but he never mentioned that day to me again.

Marion was touched by the story. It may have enabled him to drop his guard with my father. I do not recall his ever using the fake radio personality in Altoona and they talked all the time up there. They talked about country-western music, football, the Korean War, geology, aviation, Einstein, everything imaginable. They took walks. My father even took Marion to the maintenance lot – I was invited but didn't want to go – one Saturday morning to show him their earthmovers and backhoes. Marion was a charmer, but my father was too smart to fall for charm alone. There was more to it than that.

I was sure he sensed that Marion was special to me. Maybe, because of the barriers that had grown between us, he was substituting Marion for me. It is called 'displacement' in psychology. By showing me his affection for Marion, he was actually showing me his affection for me. Marion's fondness for my father was easier to figure. I think it had to do with the loss of his own dad, an economist who had worked for the World Bank, traveled the world and died young in some third world country when Marion was twelve. Marion spoke of him fondly so I knew he felt the loss.

Whatever the reasons, Marion and my father were close and I resented it. I am not proud of that; in fact, I am ashamed of it, but I felt Marion was barging in front of me, scavenging again, trying to pick up a new father. Even my mom, who coddled and complimented Marion, seemed slightly put off by the attention my father gave him.

She must have approved the invitations though. Without asking her, my father would never have suggested that Marion come up with me for Thanksgiving that year.

A month later when we were discussing Christmas, he asked me to tell Marion he would be welcome to join our family for the holidays. Both times I told him I'd pass the invitations along, but I did not.

A macabre thought occurred to me on the outskirts of Buffalo that morning as dawn struggled to lighten that forever gray sky: if I *had* invited him, things might have turned out differently. I mean who can foresee the outcomes of life's crazy chain reactions? Someone spills a bottle of milk, runs to the store for another, and is shot in a holdup. This dark idea may have occurred to me because I was tired from the drive and anxious about seeing Marion, but it occurred nonetheless, and the longer it lingered, the worse I felt. I stopped at a gas station and bought a pack of cigarettes, although I had not smoked in years. I pumped and puffed in that icy wind feeling dizzy and guilty and promised myself I would tell Marion I had always loved him. We had things to talk about, if we could.

~~~

The accident had occurred on a glorious September afternoon. Weeks later, I heard that Marion had been walking his dog in a recreation area along a bike path when a car struck him. The teenage driver and his passengers had been shouting at friends playing soccer on the adjacent field. The doctors in the trauma center believed Marion sustained two blows to the head, one as he hit the windshield, a second when he fell to the ground. They said they could not predict how much damage had been done to his brain until the intra-cranial swelling resolved, but that was a dodge probably. Their curt answers and downcast eyes told the story.

101

After six weeks he was moved to a medical floor for 'observation'; there was little more they could do. As I walked down the corridor that morning watching the room numbers drop ever closer to his, my heart sank. I intentionally passed his room looking for a bench in the hall where I could sit and collect myself. Then I heard an unfamiliar, reedy voice, "Hey, in here. Come on in." I turned around and peered in. He was sitting in a wheelchair beside his bed having his hair cut. "Come on in, dear. Want you to meet my adorable barber. Anthony, this is a dear friend from Washington, D.C. He is an authority at the National Institutes of Health on nematode reproduction." I was so relieved by this dash into his outlandish world of words and images that it brought tears to my eyes. It demonstrated that Marion not only recognized me, but his brain seemed in gear and functioning normally – for him. Despite the dire expectations and the oxygen cannula in his nose, his intro had to be good news...didn't it? I nodded at Anthony, who was removing the drape from his client's shoulders, and shook Marion's hand.

"How are you, Mare?" I said. "You look great – got an excellent haircut."

"I'm feeling good, really am. I think I'll be outta here soon."

He didn't look ill, just haggard and flaccid because he'd lost so much weight. His skin hung on him like a shirt on a hanger. It fell from his jaw in pale shrouds and from his cheekbones accentuating his eyes. The graying hair against his fair skin produced a monochromatic effect that also set off his eyes; their wide blueness cast a shadow. I

looked into those eyes needing to know what was happening behind them. I remember thinking of the phrase 'the mind's eye.' Those eyes had fronted for a quick, quirky mind that had seen the world in its own way before the accident. How that vision had been rearranged since was anybody's guess.

"Hey, get back here." I heard the snap of his fingers. "No spacing out around here. I'm spacey enough." I guess I looked at him blankly. "Don't leave me yet, my dear, you just got here."

"Oh, sorry. An all-night drive'll do that, I guess."

"So, let's go get you a coffee."

As I wheeled him down the hall to the coffee machine, nurses and orderlies greeted him. "Morning, Professor." "Have a good turkey day, Marion." One attractive woman in a beautifully tailored orange suit slowed her purposeful march down the corridor when she spotted him, leaned over, and placed a kiss gently on his cheek. I could not see his face from where I stood. I only know his immediate response was to introduce me to her as a friend who had come from Safeway Headquarters in California to judge today's synchronized grocery cart competition. "Oh, Marion, my love," she gushed, crinkling her nose and eyes at him, "you're wonderful." No changes here, I thought. He's taken over. He rolled by them all with majesty, like Prince Philip reviewing the honor guard, dispensing regal waves and empty smiles, and I was his anonymous aide-de -camp.

The mechanism that finds the balance in human relationships is a mysterious thing, like a compass but inexplicable. At the beginning two people unwittingly

assess the intangibles between them. Then, as if some magic calculus has made its shrewd computation, the balance tips and locks, and each party knows his place. Each will keep that place, follow its rules, and meet its responsibilities unless or until some critical event adjusts it. As I pushed Prince Philip back to his room precariously balancing our coffees over the handgrips of his wheelchair, I realized the balance of our relationship had not changed despite the passage of time and a brain injury. It felt as familiar as my own toothbrush, and it was the reason I had come from afar when summoned.

When a nurse's aide came to give Marion a sponge bath I went to the cafeteria for lunch and a smoke outside. I returned an hour later, hesitantly pushed open the door, and saw Marion in bed, eyes closed. The shades were drawn against the dull gray afternoon light and the ugliness of the bus terminal across the street.

"Come on in, my dear, sit down, take five minutes and tell me everything you know." I dutifully pulled up a chair, noting the term of endearment. This was new.

"Seriously, Mare," I said, trying to set the tone, "I've come all this way. Harya doon?" I asked, emphasizing an expression we had often used.

"You know, I'd really like to get out of here for an hour or two. All my stuff's in the closet – pants, shirt, 34-97's, everything. Let's go over to the bus station for a cheese daiquiri and a sandwich. Whatdaya say?"

"34-97's?"

Marion looked at me furtively then scanned the room. "Have you forgotten, man? Socks. It's the code for socks," he whispered. He was agitated, almost angry.

"Oh, yeah," I said, as if it had just come back to me. "Well, I don't think we can leave the hospital even with warm 34-97's. It's very cold out there, plus we've got your wheelchair. It would be tough..."

"Tell me, how's the Lizard? How's Petrakas and Snuffy?" These were the nicknames of old friends. A good sign, I hoped, remembering that he had not used *my* name yet. "The Lizard's finally married, you know," he said. "Tells me he's going to bring Julie up here to see me if her parole board approves the trip." A pause; he studied me, waiting for a comment, but no witty retort came to mind.

"Julie's going to finish her degree this spring. Maybe you could come down for her graduation," I said.

"Maybe..." Another pause, longer this time. Had he lost focus? Then, "What about Petrakas? Last I heard he had given up the rat race and was teaching snorkeling to elderly Elder Hostel elders in Key Largo. Zat true?"

"I don't know," I said. "The last time I spoke to him was just before he left for Seattle. Remember? His company was sending him as its liaison to Boeing?"

"Boeing, Boeing, gone! How about that," Marion's imitation of Mel Allen was perfect.

"Gone to the Keys
If you please
No coronary disease
No winter freeze
Just the life of ease.
Jeez Louise!
Well, Petrak was the smartest of all of us," his thoughts tumbled out. "Very smart fart alright. One smart fellow, he felt smart. Two smart fellows, they felt smart.

Say that five times fast. But it's the smart ones whose wheels fall off, you know, and losing a wife can do it. It'll loosen those lug nuts with quickness."

The reference was jarring. Was Marion thinking his own lug nuts were loose? "Petrakas will be fine," I assured him.

"Snuffy," Marion's attention had shifted again. "The Dempsey Dumpster of stomachs. God almighty, that guy could eat! I always envied that. You know, I've seen five volcano eruptions in my life, four World's Fairs, three Olympic games, two goat ropings, and a buzzard fuck but I've never seen anybody who could eat like the Snuff."

"I saw him in July," I said, suddenly sure that his lug nuts *were* loose. Marion was revved up but going nowhere. "He's got a good practice in Miami," I said carrying on as if all were well.

"Those were good times, weren't they, my dear? Maybe the best," he said without looking at me. He was winded. I took his hand. His eyes glazed. A minute passed, maybe two, and his breathing slowed. I shifted in my chair and watched Marion's lank face relax, then lose expression. His mouth opened. I held his hand for a long time.

~~~

"Tell me about your folks. How're things in Glocca Morra?" he said as soon as he opened his eyes, as if no time had passed, although two hours had.

"They are concerned about you. My mom told me to tell you she says a prayer for you every day and my father, well, he's worried, says as soon as they spring you, you should go to Altoona to recoup, eat good food, sleep, go for

walks, and stay as long as you want. He wanted to drive up here with me today, but with the holiday and all, I told him next time would be better."

"Your Dad's a piece of work."

"Well, you are his favorite. No doubt about it, he loves you like a son." Good start, I thought, just what I needed. "Amazing how you two connected the first time you met. Great chemistry from the start, don't you think?"

"Did you find my 37-94's?"

"No. Where are they?" I asked, forever the obedient straight man, letting another serious moment slip away.

"Everything's in the closet, man, packed and ready to go. You know, Alan hates to see me like this and it's a long drive over here for him. It'll be much better if you just take me home."

If only I could take you home, I thought. You deserve to be home; you've earned it. Since we had gone our separate ways, Marion had settled in to a good life. He had earned a doctorate in Geography, a position teaching it in the community college, and a condo he shared with his partner. I was envious.

"How is Alan?" I asked. "You know I've never met him. I've only spoken to him a couple times on the phone."

"He is a dear, my dear. This has been harder on him than on me, but he's okay. He's got family here and he leans on them." The escaped conversation about my father was still on the loose. I wanted to get back to it, but we had jumped to another good track.

"Tell me about him. How did you meet?"

"We met at the college my first week there. A couple of months later I saw him by chance at a concert. Six

hundred people there, and I saw *him*! The stars must have been aligned and as we both worked for the college it was easy to follow up." Marion reflected for a moment. He toyed with the ring on his finger and seemed soothed.

"Not to hurt your feelings, but life has been very good for me because of him," he said. "I hope *his* life's been better because of me."

"Oh, I'm sure he feels it has been, Mare," I said, although I had no idea what Alan felt. He sounded curt on the phone, had no sense of humor – so how could he appreciate Marion? – and I hated his Buffalo accent. I could not imagine what they had in common, frankly.

"From talking with him, I know how much he cares," I lied. Marion looked thoughtful, but he did not respond. "Tell me," I said, hoping to extend the conversation, "what does he do at the university?"

"He's a mechanical hedgehog. One of their very best." He stopped then and seemed to study me again. Checkmate. I was stymied and Marion fell asleep. That was typical of our conversations.

I stayed with him through Thanksgiving Day – till after midnight. I was glad I did because Alan never showed. Maybe he took the day off because he knew I was there, although he did not learn that from me. Maybe he didn't want to meet me, or maybe he never visited Marion, I don't know. Marion and I ate brown turkey, brown stuffing, brown gravy, had black coffee and brown pumpkin pie. I sat on a metal chair designed to injure backs watching Marion's uneven breathing, listening to the sounds of the unit – wobbly cart wheels and squeaky soles hauling away uneaten turkey parts and hauling in

syringes and pills, nurses' murmurs, nasal pages over the intercom – fewer and fewer as the hours passed, the white whir of machines and the ping, ping, ping of the EKG monitor. I fetched tiny cans of apple juice for Marion and me from the visitors' fridge. We clinked to Thanksgiving and the attendant came to change Marion's diaper and position. Later, the same pale lad brought Marion a diagonally halved turkey sandwich, a side of succotash, and a Styrofoam cup with warm water and a tea bag. Marion took a bite of the sandwich, held it up gingerly by its apex as if it were infectious and asked, "You know the difference between this and a box of Kleenex?"

"No, what is it?"

"There isn't much," he said without a smile.

We did converse, though, you might say. He summoned his social graces from some cranny and asked about my cat, what route I would take home, inert questions like that. And I, for what little it was worth, tried to encourage him, to persuade him that he would get better and get out because through the thickening cobwebs and labored breathing he desperately did want to get out.

Shortly before midnight, a nurse woke Marion to give him a sedative. He propped himself up supported by his elbows to swallow it. I remember him lowering himself ever so slowly back toward the bed, resisting his descent, looking out at me, imploring me to take him home. When his head sank back into the pillow his eyes closed automatically like a doll's. After a while I straightened his blankets, told him I loved him, and kissed him goodbye. His cheek was bristly and cool on my lips.

I found a motel near the hospital and fell into bed with my clothes on. Two hours later a garbage truck in the lot behind my room started emptying the motel's Dempsey Dumpsters. I could not go back to sleep after the truck roared off so I took a sedative, even though I did not know how it would react with my antidepressant. I awoke at ten in the morning feeling slightly drugged and lay there watching the news on a black and white television. Reagan had just released a letter saying he had Alzheimer's, an earthquake struck the Philippines, and Cab Calloway died. All the news was bad, it seemed. I headed slowly out of Buffalo behind a snowplow spreading sand. It was 29 degrees and sleet was flying horizontally across the bow of my rental car.

~~~

A month later I learned that Marion had died of respiratory complications. I was so depressed I was having difficulty getting out of bed to go to work. About that time, I received a manila envelope from Buffalo with no return address. It stopped me cold. I had heard nothing from Alan, although I had sent a condolence card and left a message on his answering machine. I sat down to open the envelope – I had to sit – and shakily dumped its contents onto the kitchen table. Envelopes, a dozen of them, addressed to Marion in my father's precise, mechanical draftsman's hand splayed across the tabletop. There was no note from Alan, which I found rude. This was just a house-cleaning chore for him. Anyway, there I sat like a little boy on the high diving board trying to find the courage to jump.

Those letters lay ticking like a time bomb on my table for a week. I could not open them. I wasn't sensitive about invading Marion's post-mortem privacy. Looking at my father's mail did seem sneaky and craven, but my real concern was what they would say about me. I sorted them into chronological order, stacked them neatly, and kept them in plain view on the kitchen table as a nag. Finally, on a rainy Saturday morning after putting out the garbage, making the bed, even pouring myself a Scotch, I read them. It took me an hour, awash as I was in thoughts of my dead friend holding those very letters just as I was, reveling in their attention to him; thinking also about my live father writing them – behind my back – giving Marion encouragement and the benefit of his good mind and years. It was tantalizing, even erotic in a way, spying on those men I loved, but it was frustrating too because I could hear only one voice. I read slowly and reread trying to discern Marion's half of their dialogue, imagining what he said to provoke such candor from my father, but I didn't have much luck. Even before his accident, when these letters were written, Marion was indecipherable sometimes. Finally, however, my father's letters, full of his dreams and demons, grabbed my full attention.

His first letters were simple nice-to-see-you letters with invitations to come to Altoona for Thanksgiving and Christmas, the ones I had failed to extend. I was relieved to learn Marion had received those invites and had known my parents wanted him with them for the holidays, but I winced at the hurt he must have felt knowing *I* had failed to extend their invitations. I can hardly understand that myself. He was just such a presence, warm and original

and funny, spewing strange facts. I was as bewitched by his pageant as anyone, but ... I felt obscured because he kept standing right in my parents' line of vision.

As my father became more involved in the correspondence, his remarks became more serious. They weren't exactly introspective at first, but I could catch glimpses of some second-guessing and some contrition, sentiments I had never associated with my father. He revealed another new side in discussing Marion's divorce; he was gentle and caring. "Don't look upon your marriage as <u>dishonest</u>," he wrote, with a precise line under the last word. His penmanship was even more meticulous here as he had labored for clarity. "It was an experiment, a good-faith effort that didn't hurt anyone too badly or permanently. You didn't leave a fatherless son to fend for himself or a broken-hearted woman crying herself to sleep at night. Most importantly, you and Kelly are together again and hopefully you have learned how important you are to each other."

God! He knew! He had bagged the elephant! No one had ever referred to Marion and me as a couple before! And that letter was written almost three years ago, before Marion left for Buffalo. I felt a little short of breath and my hands shook so I had to lay the letter on the table to continue reading it. "Bottom line: I'm happy for you and Kelly. You should be happy for yourselves."

I know I was happy for *my*self. My dad had been more than accepting of our relationship, he had been happy about it! He had come so far, I thought...or had he? He had always known Marion was special to me; he had taken to him right away, welcomed us in his home without

conditions or questions. Actually he had not changed at all, but in those few sentences he sure did rock my boat.

But I could sense that in his response Marion had balked at the idea of "being happy for himself" or had voiced frustrations we all feel. Even without knowing what he said, I cheered him on. "Tell him like it is, Mare! Tell him how full of hate the world is for people like us, how horrible it is to see friends die of AIDS." But the linebacker wouldn't budge. "Marion, listen," was the salutation of his next letter. "I don't know much about Nietzsche. I'm a construction guy, not a philosopher, but I know you don't have to be Superman to respect yourself, so long as you're honest. So, for God's sakes, stop feeling sorry for yourself. That's not being honest and can lead to self-contempt which you want to avoid, believe me." This didn't sound much like the tough guy I had known all my life. I was beginning to wonder who this man was and I was about to find out.

You will recall that in a previous letter my dad had mentioned "a fatherless son." That was a reference to Marion's childless state, of course, but he was referring to me too. His last letter to Marion made that clear. It was a confession, a rush of memories and introspection dashed off in pencil and lacking my dad's usual studied precision. It harked back to the day the boilers exploded at my school. Every detail of that incident, he said, remained vivid in his memory: barrel-assing in a company truck through a residential neighborhood and across someone's lawn to get to my school; the air full of rubble dust and sickish chemical smells; his skin clammy and his throat so dry he could hardly swallow. He wrote it all down: "It was

the turning point in my life, Marion. I was frantic with the fear that my boy was dead. You know, we live with this potential for random, nonsensical death every day. The 'poof factor' I call it – poof and we're gone. But, this time it was my own little Kelly's life hanging in the balance. Even though he survived, I've never been able to shake the fear that next time he might not. The fear has become an obsession and it has stunted me emotionally. I have somehow lost my ability to feel. I saw a big, dead pine tree in Florida once. It had been struck by lightning. It was upright but hollow inside. That's me, upright but empty, and most tragically, that incident left Kelly without much of a father. In your case, Marion, if you don't honor who you are, you'll just be taking another route to where I am. Don't do that – think about it. Jim."

~~~

This fervent plea that Marion not only accept who he was but be proud of it begged for his response, but that was not to be. My dad's last letter was dated three days before Marion's accident. Ironically, the 'poof factor' my dad dreaded so much had swooped down again while Marion was walking his dog that sunny September afternoon and took him from us.

I am still here, though, and I have an opportunity now, a gift from Marion, to step into their dialogue and show my dad he is not emotionally dead. I'm qualified to do this because I know him and I know how his orderly engineer's mind works. I will use his own words in his own handwriting to show him he still cares. I will remind him of the holiday invitations he sent Marion and of the Saturday morning tour he gave him of all those enormous,

yellow machines he used to maintain Pennsylvania's roads – what could be more affectionate than that?!

I'm going to set this project up to succeed. Knowing that my dad has always loved Saturday nights and my mom gets as excited as a school girl when I come home, I'm going to go to Altoona for a weekend. My dad and I will do the manly thing Saturday afternoon: we'll watch a Penn State game on TV and drink a few beers. That will loosen him up. Then he'll put on his atrocious 'Road Kill Griller' apron and use his highly technical hibachi pot to grill a steak and my mom will make Peach Melba for dessert. During dinner I will wait, crouching like a cat, ready to pounce on any segue that will allow me to turn the discussion to Marion. That shouldn't be difficult. Once there, I'm sure either my mom or dad or I will say something that will open the closet door and allow me to come out. Lastly, I'll say, "I love you both." That's my goal. I've told my mom I love her, but I've never said that to my dad and I want to.

I have had the letters for a month now. I have a good plan, but I am having trouble getting started. I have moved the letters to my bedside table right next to the phone so their presence reminds me first thing in the morning and last thing at night that I must call home to set the date for our weekend. Those damned letters nag me every time I answer the bedroom phone, and sometimes when I am alone, whether I'm at home or out, I can hear those letters – tick, tick, ticking away like that time bomb. Maybe I'll call them Saturday.

HOODWINKER

This above all else; to thine own self be true,
And it must follow, as the night the day,
Thou canst not then be false to any man.
                                        - Shakespeare

A Boy's Perspective

I was twenty-three when I learned of the sudden and mysterious dissolution of my father's friendship with Cecil, his best friend. My parents were lingering at the dining room table, sipping wine, and discussing what might have caused it. I was reading in a room nearby. I was not eavesdropping, but occasionally words drifted in my direction that carried me back to Cecil's side and private memories I associated with him: the smell of New York in his Harris Tweed jacket; his squared fingernails stained with photographic chemicals; the sprinkle of fine freckles under his eyes. I had not seen Cecil or Cynthia, his wife, since the friendship fell apart, but learning of it saddened me. It made me aware of the void his absence had left in my life and how much my parents must have missed them.

As a youngster I became so excited waiting for Cecil to arrive at our home in Connecticut that I sometimes threw up, and when he said goodbye, I always had to fight back tears. I learned so many things from him: how to pick the meat from a lobster without using utensils; how to short

sheet a bed; how to cook crepes so I could serve my mother an elegant surprise breakfast. I even grew to like the pickled herring he brought us from the Fulton Fish Market. Those chunks of raw fish submerged in brine and draped with seaweed were the least appetizing dish one could set before a fussy little boy, but I ate them enthusiastically because Cecil did.

When Cecil came to see us, the unexpected came with him. Grace, his two-door Packard convertible, was often involved in the mischief. She was a sleek, gray roadster with a maroon canvas top and many miles on her chassis, but like Cecil, she was still handsome. Cecil said she had spunk. "What's spunk, Ceese?" I asked as he turned the ignition key. "This is spunk," he said, cranking the steering wheel hard to the left and goosing the accelerator. Grace jumped sideways and wrapped herself into tight, fast circles that pinned me against the passenger door. I remained there convulsed with laughter until Cecil straightened out and drove sedately out of the parking lot.

Somehow, Cecil could make Grace's motor sputter at will. When it did, he would declare an emergency, pull to the curb, and we would jump out to perform our assigned duties. I would check the oil and lights; Cecil would tinker and mutter under the hood, mixing words like 'solenoid' and 'distributor' with an occasional 'hmmm'. Then, at a moment he deemed just right, he would ask me to turn the key in the ignition. Grace would inevitably purr sweetly back to life and we would head for the ice cream parlor to celebrate our mechanical prowess. Cecil did not believe in automatically limiting our cone intake to one apiece. Two

was better than one, if we judged the first to be of excellent quality, which we usually did. Our record was three each.

One afternoon after an emergency drill, Cecil was talking animatedly about the Yankees, our favorite team, while lowering Grace's hood. When he slammed it shut, the pointed latch that held the hood down pierced his necktie front and back, tethering him bent at the waist to the front of the car. I laughed so hard I peed a little. Cecil laughed too, but only slightly because it was hard to do in that position. Following his instructions, I eventually found the handle under the dashboard that popped the latch and freed him.

Cecil was fun and funny, but it would be misleading to portray him as a comedian. Comedians make fun of the human condition; Cecil was obsessed by how unfair it was. I remember him spending most of a weekend playing Old Maid with my little sister who had a serious case of the measles, a fever, and a deck of marked cards. The corner of the Old Maid card looked like her hamster (also named Cecil) had tried to eat it. Cecil sat at her bedside for hours, crammed into a child's chair, losing game after game. But my sister was relentless. "Just one more game, Ceese, please," she would beg and he would submit to just one more.

At the time, I wondered why he kept playing. What was in it for him? Then one night as I lay in bed, the answer came to me: Cecil was vulnerable. Of course, I did not know that word, but we kids did know that he could be deeply touched by our laughter and our tears. We loved him for that. It made him more child-like and more accessible than other adults. We had no idea it was the

heavy burden he carried that made him so sensitive to other peoples' misfortunes. Had I known, I would have understood that he really had no choice but to play Old Maid all weekend.

I am sure my family helped relieve Cecil's burden by loving him as much as we did. I believe being in my father's presence was especially reassuring to Cecil. He served as a big brother and number one fan wrapped into one. He loved Cecil's eccentricities and his style, and he envied the innocent enthusiasm with which Ceese would chase his latest dream. And yet my father's cautious nature made him incapable of such abandon. His instinct was to restrain Cecil, to protect him as he raced off to join another crusade or invest in some new venture. He was a busy guardian angel.

Despite their differences, the two men developed a unique bond. Even a little boy could sense it. I remember them during cocktail hour ambling in lockstep to the far end of our long backyard, my father's big forearm resting on Cecil's shoulder. I watched them from my bedroom window as they lounged on our deck chairs, drinks in hand, conversing as intensely as they played tennis; first one spoke, then the other, back and forth, each attentive as the other made his point, each frequently leaning forward to take an early bounce or find a better angle. Their wisecracks sent peals of laughter into the dusk and their mutual affection radiated out and touched me. I wanted to be with them and like them, but I left them alone when they were in sync like that because I sensed those moments were solemn and not to be shared by outsiders. They were the only insiders.

My Father's Perspective

My father was stretched out on his chaise longue, legs elevated for improved circulation, the morning sun warming his spare shoulders and backlighting the flyaway ends of his white hair and the blood vessels in his ears.

"So, how are you this fine morning, Pops?" I said. I lived nearby and dropped in on weekends for a morning coffee.

"Not so well, Buddy," he said. "Got to thinking about Cecil Thorne and couldn't fall asleep. Do you ever think of him?"

"Of course. I *loved* Cecil," I said. I had not seen him in decades, but the word 'love' popped out automatically.

"Well, I loved him too, son," my father countered in an emotional voice.

My father was a closet introvert. He put up a good front as an extrovert, but those who knew him well knew he was a very private person. It was out of character for him to say he had 'loved' Cecil.

In fact, that comment marked the beginning of a change in my father. Motivated perhaps by his waning strength, he became more willing to reminisce about the people who were important in his life. Cecil was at the top of the list of those he wanted us to know better. They had shared so much that for some time my father seemed torn between keeping their secrets, and letting us in on them. Eventually he broke his silence.

"Did you know I once had a Duesenberg at my disposal?" he asked one morning.

My father had an excellent memory and he told a story well. He had my attention from the beginning when he said "his" Duzzie was the J101 Model built in 1929, arguably the finest car in the world. J. Breckenridge Trulock, a big time banker whom everyone called 'the Chairman', bought one just before the stock market crashed. It was a deep maroon, such a luscious color you wanted to lick it. The Chairman hired my father, who was then in college, as his occasional chauffeur and driving instructor. They took the car out only on weekends because the Chairman was busy making money during the week. On Sunday evenings, after dropping the Chairman at his apartment, my father would park the car in its garage where it would remain during the week, except when Cecil and my father 'borrowed' it once on a Friday night.

That evening Cecil, acting as my father's chauffeur, drove him and a lady friend who did not know Cecil to a dance at the Algonquin Hotel. He dropped them there, parked the car, and returned to play his obsequious role to the hilt. All evening he loitered behind my father's chair, lighting his cigarettes, flicking dandruff from his shoulders, and whispering criticisms of the waiters to no one in particular.

When it was time to leave, my father sent Cecil to fetch the car. Forty-five minutes passed and Cecil did not reappear. Finally, he charged into the lobby out of breath. "Christ, Sir, excuse me, but I can't find the Duzzie. I don't remember where I parked it." My father was used to

dealing with Cecil's absentmindedness, so he did not panic. This was serious, though. They had misplaced...stolen actually...one of the world's most expensive cars.

"It's no wonder I couldn't sleep last night," he said. "That car cost $20,000."

But not all was lost. After putting my father's date in a cab, they started walking along the route Cecil thought he had taken, my father asking questions, Cecil looking for familiar landmarks. Suddenly he stopped; a look of relief crossed his face. He remembered deciding the Duzzie would be safest parked near a police station. Their pace increased as the headed toward the nearest one. As it came into view, they saw several cops on the sidewalk ogling the car. They strolled the remaining half block casually, nodded good evening to the policemen, and heaved sighs of relief.

When my father dropped him at his apartment, Cecil leaned in the passenger's side window, and made a confession: "You know, Bob, when I abandoned the search for the Duzzie and decided to go get you to help look, for a few minutes I couldn't remember where I'd left *you* either!"

~~~

Stories like that related more than facts. I began to see Cecil as my father saw him when their friendship was young. Cecil, who enjoyed some celebrity as a star basketball player for Columbia University, lived in a school dormitory and seldom spoke of his family. My father lived at home, but his family was seldom there. His mother, Constance, a British-born concert pianist, was devoted to

her music and to her luxuriant mane of chestnut hair. She put my father just below music on her list of priorities, but he was devoted to her perhaps because his father, George, was not. George was a construction engineer who traveled often, had weaknesses for scotch and the ladies, and a lovely tenor singing voice. He sang in saloons and Constance gave piano recitals at Carnegie Hall. That was as close as they came to having something in common.

When George met Cecil for the first time, he had a couple of shots under his belt. He entered his apartment, poured himself a drink and before my father could introduce Cecil, he began to rant about three 'lazy colored boys' he had just fired. Neither Cecil nor my father said a word. My father knew it would have been useless and Cecil was struggling to control his temper. After two minutes of George's harangue, Cecil marched out of the apartment without saying a word. His face was beet red and he slammed the heavy front door so hard the barometer fell from the wall.

This incident was one of several my father had witnessed in which Cecil's anger had prevailed over his better judgment. My father knew Cecil was quick to perceive an insult, found it difficult to forgive one, and was prone to hear one when none was intended. When asked about his flare-ups Cecil always gave the same, uninformative response: "The Devil made me do it." He was good at building walls.

Cecil said little about his own family. My father knew only that Cecil's father was dead and his mother, an American Indian, had gone home to live in Council Bluffs, Iowa, after her husband's death. When she visited New

York once, Cecil took Bob to her hotel to introduce them. My father remembered vividly his first impression of her. Her blue-black hair, penetrating hazel eyes, and copper skin were "stunning", he said, and her cool demeanor and regal posture demanded that he give her his full attention. They drank coffee into the late afternoon and spoke of serious matters: the stock market, crime, Babe Ruth's ethnicity, Indian rights, etc. My father focused on thinking clearly and speaking well because he was sure Mrs. Thorne was using her considerable intellect and her beauty to assess the man her son was calling his 'best friend'. When the time came for him to leave, my father felt drained, but full of admiration for her because she had shown such dedication to her son. As she said goodbye she called him Robert for the first time. He considered that a sign the interview had gone well.

During the following year, my father inquired about her occasionally until one day Cecil told him gently he had just learned of her death in a car accident out west. My father was stunned and offered Cecil his condolences, but that evening an unsettling thought occurred to him: Cecil really had not seemed much affected by his mother's death. The impression disturbed my father for weeks.

In looking back on their adventures, my father was also disturbed that he once helped Cecil and Cyn get an abortion. "I knuckled under too quickly," he said. The first sign of trouble, he explained, occurred one morning after a tennis match. Cecil sat down heavily on a park bench and buried his face in his hands. My father sat beside him and put a hand on his shoulder. They sat for some time, alone among the many passersby, silent within the din of the

city. Finally, Cecil regained his composure and said without looking at his friend, "Cyn's pregnant."

My father, who was good in a crisis, figured the best way to comfort Cecil would be to offer him a reassuring plan. "Okay, let me think," my father said, his hand still on Cecil's shoulder. Cecil gave him some time. "Ceese, don't despair. I think we have a couple good options," my father said. "We can either keep the wedding date as is and have the baby seven months after you're married, which wouldn't upset any of your friends, or we could move the date forward and have the baby nine months after the wedding." He felt pleased with his succinct analysis but Cecil, whose face was dark with intensity and streaked with sweat and tears, shot back, "Goddamit, Bob, we're not *having* a baby! So, are you going to help me or not?"

"Yes, Ceese, of course I am," he said, without knowing if he could keep his promise. Chairman Trulock, the banker, helped him keep his word. He put my father in touch with an acquaintance who knew a doctor who performed abortions because he believed some women need this 'last option.' He was selective and secretive about this practice, and my father was equally discreet. He researched the doctor's record and asked to see where he worked. The doc wanted to meet the parents. My father said, "Only when we have an agreement." They went back and forth and when they finally reached an understanding, Cynthia balked.

My father said he was never privy to Cecil and Cyn's discussions, but he spent hours with Cecil during the next few days. Cecil was terrified by the idea of fatherhood. "I can't do this, Bob," he said repeatedly. "I'm not ready. It's

too risky." He could not sleep, his stomach was upset, and he smelled bad. One morning Constance, my grandmother, took Cecil's hand, walked him into the bathroom, pointed at the bath she had drawn for him, and ordered him to bathe. She had seldom shown such a display of maternal care.

His appearance did not concern my father so much as his fear of fatherhood did. That was so irrational it made him wonder about Cecil's grasp of reality. Cecil was a natural with kids; he reveled in their company. Every time they played tennis a big bunch of his little fans appeared from somewhere to cheer for him. Thinking back to how much I loved Cecil as a boy, I agreed completely with my father: Cecil was designed for fatherhood.

Cynthia used every ploy imaginable to change Cecil's mind, but to no avail. Finally, she acquiesced. After the abortion, she told my father she had had to decide whom she wanted more, Cecil or the baby, an impossibly cruel choice, and she wondered if she would ever feel comfortable with her decision.

Sixty years after this event my father still kicked himself for not having discussed Cecil's fatherhood phobia with him. "We really should have discussed it at length. We should have stayed up into the wee hours for as long as it took." he said. "Who knows, we might have been able to get to the bottom of it and Ceese might have been a father all these years. But, back then men were not supposed to have heart-to-heart talks about their feelings," he pointed out. "We were supposed to be stoic ... the strong, silent types. As a result, we ignored a critical moment in Cecil's life. It was a bad mistake."

127

At 85, my father's body was wearing out. His mind remained clear, though, and I think he was trying to use it to tie up some of his life's loose ends. One afternoon, after watching tennis on television, he said, "Despite all Cecil put me through, I'm glad I knew him. I only wish I knew what alienated him." This wistful comment led him to relive one last time their final luncheon and sift through his memories of it for clues that might enlighten him.

In 1955, my father had just come east after a three-year business venture in Los Angeles. For their reunion luncheon, he selected a restaurant known for its decorum and wealthy clientele. Curiously, Cecil, who always dressed impeccably, arrived with an open collar, a loosened tie, and a barn door rip in the knee of one pant leg. He made no mention of his appearance, but quickly turned the conversation to civil rights in New York City.

The racial cauldron was boiling in 1955. The previous year the Supreme Court had shaken the country with its Brown vs. the Board of Education decision and Rosa Parks had inspired many others, black and white, to get involved in the Civil Rights Movement. Churches were burned, Freedom Riders killed, and the KKK defended their "for whites only" water fountains and bathrooms with German shepherds and lynch mobs. Cecil was caught up in the Movement. "I'm ready now to fight with my brothers for our rights, Bob," he said gesturing at his ripped pants. "I'm ready!"

Cecil's phrases "my brothers" and "our rights" did not escape my father's notice. "You sound like you're playing for their team already," my father commented.

"I'm playing for *our* team, Bob. I'm glad you're finally hearing me." My father was not taking Cecil's comments at face value, though. He attributed them to Cecil's enthusiasm for the cause and his inclination to hop aboard a passing bandwagon now and then just for fun. The problem was that my father found this bandwagon un-American, which put him often at odds with his friend. When, in response to some incredible claim Cecil made, he heard himself say in exasperation, "Cecil, don't be ridiculous ..." it dawned on him that he had better tread lightly. Their friendship had been untended and untested for three years. My father did not want to overburden it, so for the remainder of their luncheon he mostly listened, chose his words carefully, and kept his emotions in check.

"I must have said or done something because we never spoke again," he said. "Your mother and I called, sent invitations, birthday presents...never had a reply." He looked tired. "Whatever I did, it beats the hell out of me," he said with a New York shrug of his thin shoulders, and within minutes, he was asleep on his chaise longue.

Two weeks later, my father died peacefully at home. While sorting through his things, I found in his bedside table a vintage photo of him and Cecil in their tennis whites on a court surrounded by tall buildings. I had it framed and kept it on my chest of drawers until I went to see Cecil in New York two years later.

Cecil's Perspective

One October night, while checking into a hotel in New York, I noticed a Manhattan phone book on the counter. I

flipped through the pages to Thorne and found four Cecils. Good odds, I thought, wondering if he were still alive. Impulsively, while the clerk was busy with a defective room key, I decided to call. My Cecil would have been in his early 80's then. I dialed the first number. I recognized instantly the distinctive voice and the accent, a mixture of sophistication and the New York street. "Hello, Ceese." I said, "This is Buddy, a voice from your past." There was a brief pause and the voice replied, "I'm so happy to hear from you." His greeting dispelled my concerns that he might have forgotten me or had no interest in talking to me. "You can't imagine how much this means to me," he said, his voice filled with emotion. "Why don't you come visit? I'm dying to play a few hands of Old Maid."

"Only if I can bring the cards," I replied. Ceese chuckled. We rambled through some questions and answers. It was comfortable conversation, but I detected melancholy in his voice. He was reluctant to hang up, and he urged me to come see him. "I have things to tell you," he said.

A month later on a cold, gray morning my sister Connie and I met at Grand Central Station and took a cab to Cecil's apartment. The elevator clanked and climbed to the 12th floor. We exchanged no words, only sterile smiles to cover the emotions we were feeling. We followed the numbers to his apartment, pushed the doorbell, and waited. When at last we faced each other across the threshold, my sister flung open her arms. It was spontaneous, she told me later. It was the perfect greeting. Cecil moved gracefully into her embrace. I watched him close his eyes and savor her affection. It made me wonder

how long he had been without human contact, as my parents had heard that Cynthia had died several years earlier.

Despite minor age-related changes, I would have recognized him anywhere. His dark hair, silver now, was still combed straight back, except for a lock that fell fashionably across his forehead. He was thinner and darker, but his skin was smooth, no jowls, neck folds, or wrinkles, save at the corners of his eyes. The face suggested a mix of ethnicities: his mother's Indian blood in the straight nose and high cheekbones; perhaps a touch of Mediterranean or even Arab blood in the olive skin. My mother said she – and many other women – found his face "alluring." Only the eyes had changed appreciably. Those dark eyes, the essence of his charm, would not hold my gaze for long. The melancholy I had heard on the phone I saw in his eyes. "You look like you could still start at guard for Columbia, Ceese," I said, preferring banalities so early in our visit.

Indeed Cecil did look great. He had always had exceptional taste and style and had dressed with imagination. He greeted us that day in dungarees, loafers, a black turtleneck, and a deep purple vest he said was woven in Finland. He looked like he had just come from one of his Vogue fashion shoots.

Cecil poured coffee, set out some cookies, and we settled down in the living room to renew our acquaintance.

"Did you know my dad went to Dartmouth on a four-year lacrosse scholarship?" he asked out of the blue. "He loved living up there and wanted to stay in New England after graduation, but couldn't find work so he returned to

New York and took a job as a clerk with a bank in Brooklyn."

"Do you remember him, Ceese?" I asked. "Didn't he die when you were young?"

"No, he died about 20 years ago down in Florida ... a broken man."

"How so?"

"The poor guy never stopped expecting he'd get what he deserved but he never got it. I used to overhear him complaining to Mom that the bank promised him this, promised him that, but they broke every promise. So, he left; ended up as a bookkeeper for a firm in Brooklyn." While I was taken aback by the heat in Cecil's voice, my sister stepped in and asked, "But was he a good dad, Ceese?"

"Yes, he was. He and Mom sheltered us from the abuse he took at work and he wouldn't let his three brothers get started with their stories either."

"But I thought your Mom moved back west after your Dad died."

"No, she lived here right up to her death in Brooklyn at 90 years of age." Why'd you think that?"

"Because my father told me all about her. He said she was gorgeous, smart, somewhat intimidating, and was killed in a car crash out west." Cecil did not reply.

"I'm confused, Ceese..." was all I could say before he interrupted.

"Let me tell you about her. She was all the things your dad said; she just didn't die out west. Early on, she wanted to meet your dad because I talked about him all the time. Actually, I think she was worried that he was a gambler or

a rackets man targeting me because I was a pretty good college basketball player. How well I played could affect the odds. Anyway, it was impossible to take him over to my family's house, so she rented a hotel room and I brought Bob there."

"But...did you tell him she'd died?" I asked.

"It was an awful thing to do, I know, but they really hit it off in the hotel. Bob was smitten and Mom impressed and I was really worried she might spill the beans if they met again."

At that moment, an alarm clock rang in the kitchen and Cecil excused himself. "Gotta take my medicine," he said. When he was out of earshot, I whispered to my sister, "Did that make sense to you?"

"We're missing something," she whispered back.

He returned immediately and apologized. "I fell last week. Ended up in the hospital for three days."

"Oh, Ceese. How come?" my sister asked.

"A little arrhythmia," he said. "But let me tell you what happened in there. A nurse who took care of me scared me to death when she discharged me. She took me down to the street in a wheelchair, and as she helped me into the cab, she took my hand in hers, put her face close to my ear and said, 'Don't you worry, Mr. Thorne, nobody's gonna find out. You're safe.' "I have no idea how she knew," Cecil said.

"Knew what, Ceese? You had no idea she knew what?" my sister repeated.

Cecil pushed back against his chair, closed his eyes, and ran his fingers through his hair. Then he leaned forward forearms on his thighs, head down, eyes focused

on the carpet. "Didn't your father tell you?" he asked, glancing up at us.

"Tell us what?"

Cecil hesitated one last time and said quietly, "I'm a Negro."

The words sucked the air out of the room. No one moved or spoke. Finally, I said stupidly, "What do you mean? You're a colored man?" Cecil nodded. I glanced at Connie. She sat stunned.

"You never told Dad?" I asked.

"Yeah, I told him back in the mid-50's just after he came back from California. First and only time I had told anyone and it was not easy, believe me. For months, I debated whether I should tell him. I realized I had broken the trust between us by lying to him for years so I figured, at first, he could never forgive me and I decided not to tell him."

My sister and I sat in silence.

"But then I thought, hoped really, that Bob might support my decision to 'pass,' as they say, if I could just explain my rationale to him. So I talked to him about how hard it was to be successful in photography. I told him the white editors keep all the good assignments from the few Negroes in the business. I kept thinking of my dad. He had an Ivy League education and a work ethic than made him an All-American lacrosse player and yet they wouldn't promote him from office boy!"

Cecil had still not said exactly what he told Bob. He kept wandering away from that detail. So, when he paused for a sip of cold coffee I asked, "Did you actually tell Dad?"

"Yes, I had to because I wanted his approval for what I had done, but I figured he needed to understand first why I'd done it." Cecil was repeating himself, procrastinating. "I thought he might actually admire my decision. After all, it takes some courage to give up your family and your heritage to be free, don't you think?"

Neither my sister nor I answered. Sensing Cecil was on the brink of telling us what he said to our Dad, we waited. But when he began to ramble again, I took a different tack. "When you told him, how did he respond?" I asked.

A strange expression crossed Cecil's face. "I remember the exact words," he said in a tight voice. "When I tried to tell him I was a Negro, he said, 'Oh, Cecil, don't be ridiculous.'"

He made an attempt to continue, but could not. He tried to take a sip from his empty coffee cup, then got up to turn on some lights. He stooped slowly near a table lamp and his hand trembled as he reached for the switch. The Vogue model had become an old man.

"You know he didn't mean to hurt you, Ceese," my sister said into the silence.

"Con, he dismissed my life in three words."

"But are you sure he understood what you were saying?"

Cecil leaned forward into his response. "Don't be ridiculous," he repeated those poisonous words. "That meant he thought I was making it up, or that I'd lost my mind. What else could it mean?" he snapped, looking at Connie. But Cecil was not soliciting answers. He had them and delivered them with such precision it was clear he had been thinking about them for years. "On the other hand, if

he did believe I was colored, it meant he considered me ridiculous for having betrayed my race just for a better chance at career advancement. Or, maybe he thought I was cowardly for crossing over just to avoid the bigotry my dad endured for years; or, that I was stupid to have lived a lie all these years just so I didn't have to live in the black ghetto. Maybe I was ridiculous, but for Bob of all people to have judged me that way..."

"Ceese, let me tell you something," I said. "Toward the end of his life my father talked more about you than anyone else. Two weeks before he died, he told me he loved you like a brother. That's the truth." I was talking fast, hoping to right my father's reputation in Cecil's eyes without implying that Cecil had judged him wrongly. "He could not have imagined how difficult it has been for you to live your life, but he would have been so proud of your accomplishments. You are a well-known fashion and portrait photographer, Ceese. Your portrait of Hemingway is all over the bookstores now. You've made it. Don't these facts justify your decisions and your sacrifices?"

"No they don't," he said, "and I'm not sure Bob would have been impressed. I didn't blaze a trail for others to follow. I hid my trail so nobody could find it. I hoodwinked everyone I knew. And do you know why? Because I was afraid somebody would discover I had lived a lie and make me pay for it. The truth is I've been letting people take advantage of me for years because I've been terrified that I'd be discovered. That's why I didn't even tell Cynthia."

Silence descended again. I remember hearing an occasional taxi horn from the streets far below and my breathing – nothing else. Cecil lay sprawled on the sofa, as

if his announcement had blown him backward. My sister sat stunned again and I just stared at Cecil, wondering if it were true. Because I felt so uncomfortable I said, "Ceese, are you sure you want to talk about this?"

"Yes, I am sure." My sister got up from her chair and sat down next to him. He righted himself from his slouch and put his hand on hers. "I debated this forever," he began. "It was the worst period of my life. I even met my dad once to get his input, but that was a waste! He thought my decision to 'pass' was smart and he envied my life as a white man because he never appreciated how lonely it was to be isolated from the family, or how vigilant I had to be to live my 'white' life. He never listened when I told him how constant the pull was to cross back over so I could be myself again, so I could stop feeling I had betrayed my race." He paused briefly and looked at us for support. Then he repeated his father's final advice, "If you can satisfy yourself that Cynthia's not a racist, marry her, and God bless you both – but always keep your secret!"

"That's pretty cold advice, pretty cynical. Didn't he even ask if you loved each other?" my sister asked.

"No time for that," Cecil replied. "The situation got worse fast." Cecil hesitated briefly, took a deep breath, and plunged on. "Cyn got pregnant right after we got engaged."

"Oh, God, Ceese. I don't know if I can stand this," I interrupted, but it made him smile for the first time that afternoon.

"Do you know why I didn't tell her? It's so simple! Because I just couldn't see myself sitting down with the poor girl, as upset as she was then, and saying to her, "By the way, Hon, I'm a Negro."

The line made me giggle. Then my sister started. Cecil looked quizzical momentarily, and he began to laugh. One laugh begot another. For several minutes, we laughed uncontrollably; we laughed until the tension eased and we had no more tears.

Cecil pulled us back to reality, though, even as he wiped his cheeks. "I should have told her," he said. "We could have handled it together." He looked so forlorn; suddenly, I was overcome with sadness. Cecil continued. "By keeping my secret from her at that critical moment I was withholding an offer of trust. She really deserved better."

"Ceese, you're beating yourself up," I said. "You had a long, happy marriage. There are too many variables for you to say a different decision would have given you a better life."

"No. If she'd known, she'd have loved me anyway. It would have made us stronger," he insisted. He thought for a moment and added the *coup de grace*, "In a way, I think my decision condemned us to live separate lives forever."

My sister squeezed Cecil's hand and said, "I remember Cyn as a happy person. I am sure she didn't feel separated from you."

"I hope not, God rest her soul. She was a good woman, not a bigot like my dad suspected, but she was high-strung and I didn't want to see her hit with the hatred she would have faced back then as the mother of a black baby. Even if she had produced a baby as white as I look, those black genes would have been there ready to strike the next generation." Cecil stopped for a moment. We listened to the silence while he thought. "I forced Cyn to do it, you

know – to have the abortion," he said. "She was totally opposed to it."

My sister took his hand again and said. "Oh God, Ceese! Oh my God!" He found it difficult to speak but acknowledged her kindness with a glance.

"One more thing...to make this complete," he said. "I did promise myself that if we survived the abortion ordeal, I would come clean with Cyn. I would introduce her to my family so she could decide about marriage with all the facts. Most of my family thought I was better off as a white man so I was sure they would welcome her into the family. But I broke my promise to myself, I'm sorry to say. I never introduced her to them, never told her about them. I never gave her a chance... or them."

By the time Cecil ended his soliloquy, night had fallen. My sister had wrapped herself in a blanket more to fend off additional heartache than to dispel the chill in Cecil's apartment. I felt spent. My hands shook as I carried our coffee cups to the kitchen, and my shoulders and neck ached. Cecil had stopped talking. He seemed – and perhaps he felt – vulnerable after revealing so much of himself. I expected him to apologize, but he did not, which I hoped meant that he had no regrets. As he stood at the sink rinsing the dishes, my sister walked over to him, put her arm around his waist, and told him she was proud of him. At that moment, I snuck into Cecil's bedroom and left the vintage photograph of 'the boys' in their tennis whites on his chest of drawers.

We put on our warm coats and walked two blocks in a bitter wind to Praiano's Pub. Its warmth and bustle was a welcome change from the empty sidewalks. When the

owner spotted Cecil, he led us to a booth in the corner. "I saved your table, Mr. Thorne," he said, shaking Cecil's hand. "I'll be right back with food." On the wall above the booth hung a framed page from the *New York Times*, dated November 1928, with a photo of a familiar, trim figure suspended near the hoop about to score. The headline read: "Columbia Clips Crimson for Championship – Thorne Scores 22."

Tony brought appetizers, wine, and a piping hot ravioli dish. The food seemed to energize Cecil because he set out again for the past, but this time, perhaps due to fatigue or wine, he lost his way. He drifted into a murky monologue, in which he insisted, in a conspiratorial voice, that his life depended upon his maintaining the integrity of his white status. He demanded that we swear never to mention his secret to anyone.

"You see, I am surrounded by competitors who have been jealous of me for years," he said. "If they knew I'd been 'passing' all this time, there's no telling what they might do. And some members of my own family who know I've been 'passing' hate me for it. That's why I seldom visit my relatives and only at night," he said in a whisper. "That's why I didn't go to see my mother before she died and why I'm really concerned for my life these days." Cecil sat with his elbows on the table, his hands clasped tightly above his untouched food. His face was flushed with anger.

"Ceese, why don't you have a sip of wine?" I said raising my glass. "And some of your ravioli? It's delicious. You're safe now and with friends." He stared at me, a lost look in his eye, and for a moment, I did not know if he

would explode at me or take a deep breath and relax. Cecil had told us how debilitating it had been over the decades to feel vulnerable and alone all the time and how unrelenting the stresses of maintaining his white identity had been. That night we witnessed the toll those lonely, stressful years had taken.

"You're right," he said, his voice sounding more normal. "Enough of this for today. You all have been a Godsend." The three of us raised our glasses and drank a toast to our next get-together.

After dinner, we walked Cecil home, my sister on his right arm, I on his left. We walked in silence and slowly to postpone saying our farewells and we huddled together to share our warmth and because we felt close. We rode up to the 12th floor and traipsed down the empty corridor with our arms still around each other. At Cecil's door, we lingered trying to find words to express how we felt, but they would not come. At last, we managed to say goodbye, but not to stifle a tear or two in the old elevator as it brought us down to a shaky landing.

Post Script

We spoke by phone regularly for half a year after our visit, insignificant but affable conversations, but there was to be no next get-together. I called one day, heard a nasal recording say, "This line is no longer in service," and knew he was gone. A week later, I saw his obituary in the *Times*. I cut it out and put it on our refrigerator door with a magnet. It was fitting to preserve Cecil's memory by

surrounding his obituary with photos of our family, mostly kids.

A year after his death, my sister and her family spent Christmas with us. One night after everyone had gone to bed, I found her standing in front of the obituary looking pensive. "A penny for your thoughts," I said.

"Let's pull that sad obituary down and replace it with this," she said. In one quick shuffle, she slid the article from under its magnet and handed me a red and green envelope. Inside I found a copy of that black and white photo of 'the boys' solemnly posed yet dashing in their old-fashioned tennis costumes. I placed it in the middle of the Kodachrome array on our refrigerator door. It remains there to this day. Some folks, I'm sure, think that old photo looks out of place among those happy faces and informal poses, but those folks do not know the story. They do not know that Cecil had been out of place most of his life, except when he was among children.

MELON FOR MAID SERVICE

Dulles Airport was pure frenzy, a tangle of languages, tension, and motion. Travelers coursed toward their gates hauling carry-ons and worried looks. Others sat fidgety, talking on cells, thumbing magazines, listening for yet another nasal announcement: the departure of Flight 234 is delayed due to severe thunderstorms. Rain pounded the tarmac and ran down the concourse windows like endless tears.

Fast forward twenty travel hours: I am running alone along a lane in rural Japan in late afternoon light, in sweet air scented with pine and fertile earth. I hear only my footfall, my breathing, and the delicate duet of a breeze humming in the pines and insects chirping rhythmically. Recalling my Dad's mantra to 'stop and smell the roses' I slow then stand still to savor the serenity before me. A meticulous patchwork of gray-green rice paddies extends to a stand of stately trees in the distance. Miniature figures, bent like commas, wearing baggy blue pants and conical hats, are transplanting rice seedlings. The shallows before them, where they have sown, sprout green stubble; the marsh behind them is unblemished, a quicksilver mirror awaiting their baby steps and fingertip plantings. In my sleep-deprived mind, the scene registers mystically

as if through gossamer. I am uncertain whether the chaos of Dulles yesterday or the beauty of the moment is more surreal.

I had flown to Narita airport, well outside Tokyo, en route to Jakarta. Since my connecting flight did not leave until the next day, I had taken a shuttle to my hotel. The ride seemed endless, but drugged with fatigue, I was beyond impatience. As I swayed along, I was dreamily pleased by how rural the landscape was becoming. Upon arrival, I awakened to see that my hotel stood virtually alone in the countryside. No malls, sirens or throbbing neon. No gas stations, diesel fumes or whining tires. Just farmland, birds, and fresh air.

After checking in, I pull on my running gear and head out for an attempt at rejuvenation. It is too early to sleep in this distant time zone, and I am ready to see Japan. A run in a new place seems to put me in touch with it, lets us rub shoulders. I run along flat, dirt roads bearing left at intersections hoping to trace a loop back to my hotel. I run past azaleas in long ranks of ochre and lavender bordering the paddies. I draw stares from women in the fields protected from the elements by old-fashioned bonnets, long-sleeved smocks, and high rubber boots. The orderliness seems obsessive. Even machinery parked for the night appears to be tucked away artfully.

About two miles from home, I come upon a weathered wooden hut framed by two gnarled evergreens. Before the hut two worn trestle tables, their wide planks graying and soft as cat's fur, offer displays of luscious fruits and vegetables. I pull in, sweaty and salivating, and spy a stack of watermelon wedges on a small table inside the hut. I

take one, assuming it is a free sample, then another. I smile appreciatively at the ancient proprietor watching me from his chair. He stands and bows when I smile. Too late, I think maybe the wedges are not free. I dig into my key pocket where I had stashed 100 yen for an emergency and offer it to him. He bows again solemnly then with a toothy grin points to the melon. I nod and expend my only Japanese word, "*Konichiwa*?" – "How are you?" He bows and hands me a football-sized watermelon. I bow. He hands me change and bows again. I bow one final time, caught up in the ceremony. Six bows and change and I have purchased a melon!

I head for the hotel, the melon tucked under my arm, running like Walter Peyton. In those immaculate surroundings, where each seedling and sluice is perfectly placed, tossing the melon to the side of the road seemed unthinkable. It would have been like dumping garbage. So, I carry it to my room where I leave it next morning: melon for maid service.

CONSEQUENCES

Early on the morning of 13 July 1917, twelve pilots assigned to Home Defense Squadron-37 at Stow Maries Aerodrome in Essex, England, abandoned their breakfasts, pulled on their bulky flight overalls, and ran for their Sopwith Pups. They had just heard from spotters on the coast that five Zeppelin bombers had crossed the North Sea and turned south. HDS-37's mission was to intercept the Germans and shoot them out of the sky before they could drop their 110-pound high explosive bombs on the City of London.

Because Adam "Adie" Scott, an American rookie, was the last to take-off, there were no airborne eyewitnesses to report what happened, but Adie's crew chief was watching from his redoubt near the end of the runway. He said Adie was late lifting off, probably because he had never coaxed an aeroplane laden with a full fuel load – 600 pounds – into the air. He speculated that Adie had pulled his nose up a touch too far as he became more desperate to clear the trees beyond the runway. This may well have stalled the aeroplane and, at an altitude of 200 feet or less, there was no room to recover. The thunderous explosion shattered windows in the Officers' Mess where Adie had taken his last meal less than fifteen minutes before.

~~~

Jane Scott, Adie's mother, was an elegant but edgy lady whose health had always been delicate. She had begged Adie's father, C.K. Scott, to forbid their son from

going to military flying school because that inevitably would mean going to war where his life would be at risk. Everything had played out just as she had feared: flight school in Canada, assignment in England, and then. . . When she heard her doorbell ring at eight o'clock that morning, she knew her life would never be the same. Upon finding the courage to open the front door, she encountered two uniformed soldiers, their young faces ill at ease with the grief they were about to deliver. As one of them handed her the dreaded telegram, Mrs. Scott threw a hand across her mouth, sank to her knees without a sound, and pitched forward in a dead faint.

Adie's hometown of Spencer, New York, was a prosperous village of almost 5,000 people, but its traditions and structure made it seem smaller. Its daily newspaper kept residents informed of each other's achievements and failures, and the summer park concerts and winter snow sculpture competition gave them opportunities to mingle and reacquaint. Just a year ago, Adie himself had helped stoke village spirit by leading the high school baseball team to a state championship.

As word of his death raced over the phone lines and along the streets of Spencer, the village seemed to stumble from the impact of the news. Some stores closed. Women wept in the streets and hugged each other. Men, who never drank during the week, popped into their favorite bars to take solace in a couple of beers and exchange recollections of the talented, good-looking boy who was Spencer's first casualty of the Great War.

Nellie Knight, Adie's high school sweetheart, was studying nursing at Spencer Hospital. She was a striking

young woman with a patrician face, a strong nose, and a high forehead. Her serious, grey-blue eyes were the color of an early morning sky and conveyed a degree of self-assurance and poise seldom seen in a person her age. Nellie was called into her supervisor's office that afternoon and informed of Adie's death. She felt faint initially, then sick, just as she had when she learned of her father's death.

She asked for permission to leave the hospital without knowing where she would go, but found herself heading for Adie's parents' home, her mind darting from thought to thought as she moved along the sidewalks in a daze. She stopped once, feeling nauseated. *They invested so much love in him and derived so much joy from him. How will they live with this loss?* She remembered Adie bounding into the kitchen to greet his father one day after school. "Hi, Papa," he said, then kissed him on the cheek, mussed his hair, and snatched his remaining half cookie all in one motion. Mr. Scott beamed. They looked so happy to see each other that Nellie felt she had intruded on an intimate moment. *There would be no more such moments for father or son.* The first time Adie kissed her they were in the Scotts' kitchen and afterward he danced around the table saying how much he had wanted to do that. *Never again would she feel his touch.* Nellie recalled his animated, handsome face – curly, reddish-brown hair, hazel eyes, and his broad grin that appeared so quickly it was always a surprise. *Never to be seen again.*

When Nellie arrived at the Scotts' handsome Tudor home, several cars were parked in front. Mr. Scott answered the door. "Nellie, my dear, come in. How are

you?" he asked stepping back into the vestibule. Nellie was shocked: although he had received the news only hours earlier, he already looked twenty years older. His skin was pallid, his posture, stooped, and his kind, perceptive eyes had little expression.

"I'm sick at heart," she said in a shaky voice. Mr. Scott opened his arms in consolation. She leaned up and kissed him on the cheek.

"And how are *you*?"

"I'll survive," he said in a flat voice.

"And Mrs. Scott?"

"She's in shock and in bed. The doctor gave her a sedative."

"She'll survive too," Nellie said with a sad smile. "I know this is not a good time. You have a wife and guests to look after and I should be at work. But may I come visit again in a week or two?"

"Please do. I want to talk to you, Nell." She took it as a sincere request and promised to call him soon.

She took both his hands in hers and was surprised to hear herself say, "You know I loved him."

"I know," he managed to reply.

~~~

Two weeks later, Mr. Scott and Nellie found themselves leaving St. Mark's Church together after the early service. As his house was on the way to hers, they walked together for several blocks. When their conversation waned momentarily, Mr. Scott said, "Do you have time for a cup of coffee? Mrs. Scott's still in bed and I would love some company."

"Yes, I have time," Nellie, said.

He opened the door for her and led the way saying, "The kitchen is for family. Let's sit in there." He shucked off his shoes and loosened his tie while making a pot of coffee. *How strange to be here without Adie, talking about him with his father.* She recalled feeling intimidated by Mr. Scott the first time they met because of his reputation as a wealthy genius. He had invented and patented a process for waxing cardboard. With his innovation, he had introduced mankind to the milk carton, revolutionized the food packaging industry, and made himself financially secure for life. He had put Nellie at ease by serving her molasses cookies with milk and they had chatted mostly about France. "I felt comfortable with him," she told her mother that evening, "but then it's difficult to be cowed by a man who is sharing cookies and milk with you. What do you think of him, Mother?"

Her mother had responded cryptically, "He's a rare bird."

Mr. Scott, interrupting Nellie's reverie, poured her coffee and asked, "Didn't we have cookies around this table the first time we met?" She smiled at the synchronicity of their thoughts. He folded his tall frame into a kitchen chair and they talked for almost two hours. Mostly they shared stories about Adie and, in doing so, they shared their grief. Nellie went home feeling as if she had made a friend.

As a result of their visit, Nellie saw Mr. Scott in a new light. His swarthy complexion, craggy features and unruly hair no longer seemed coarse; rather, they lent character and intelligence to his face. Instead of shyness and reserve in his deep-set brown eyes, she saw calmness and

151

confidence. Her new perception of him reminded her of something her mother told her: "All my friends are good-looking," she said, "because I see in them all the beautiful qualities that make them my friends."

Three weeks after their first meeting, Mr. Scott called and invited Nellie for coffee after church again. "I have a question for you," he announced as they set out on the walk to his home. "I've been wondering what ever prompted Adie to turn his sights from college to flying? Do you know how that happened?"

"Yes, I think I do," Nellie said and described an airshow they had attended a year earlier. "It started with the deep growl of an aeroplane engine filling the sky and an announcer saying, 'Ladies and Gentlemen, our first maneuver will be the deadly 'inverted loop.''" A second later, every bystander either screamed or ducked impulsively as a bright red biplane, approaching from behind, skimmed over them at about fifty feet. Simultaneously, the pilot gave his plane full throttle and yanked it into a vertical climb. The engine screamed as it shot up toward the clouds, but the higher it climbed, the slower it went, and the harder its engine labored. Nellie said she worried it was going to stall and drop backward out of the sky onto them. "I was scared to death," she told Mr. Scott. Fortunately, at the last instant, the nose tipped beyond vertical and for a brief moment that red plane hung motionless, silent, and upside down against the blue sky. Then it began its inverted fall toward earth, gaining momentum quickly until it was plummeting toward the crowd at 200 mph. Once again, Nellie felt sick with fear. She could not imagine how the pilot would be able to avoid

plunging into them, but he did. He pulled out of his dive just above the tree tops, performed a couple more maneuvers, and landed light as a sparrow, near where they stood. After the show, Nellie's legs were weak and her hands were shaking, but Adie was exhilarated to have witnessed such expert flying. He ran to the plane and engaged the pilot in a long conversation "The bug really bit him that afternoon," she told Mr. Scott. "That barnstormer did it. He was not only a showman, but he really knew how to fly too." Later that week while walking home from school, Adie made an announcement: "I've decided I'm going learn how to fly the fastest planes in the world, Nellie. That's my goal and that's what I'm going to do."

"Why didn't he tell me about it?" Mr. Scott wondered aloud.

"Because he didn't want you and Mrs. Scott to worry. . . and he was right. That pilot was killed just two weeks after we saw him." Mr. Scott sat in silence. "I wish I hadn't gone that day," Nellie whispered.

"Why?"

"Because that airshow led him directly. . . to his death. He met a master and was inspired by him and I did nothing about it. I should have found a way to stop him."

Mr. Scott sat deep in thought. Finally he said, "It was Adie's decision, Nell. He had an almost pathological sense of competition. It would not surprise me if he saw combat flying as a test he wanted to take. I used every persuasive skill I have to convince him his education was of foremost importance. But, nothing worked. Don't blame yourself."

"You are kind, Mr. Scott," but she felt guilty and shook her head in disagreement.

~~~

Over the winter and spring, Mr. Scott and Nellie met every month or so. Nellie sensed that their talks about Adie were therapeutic for Mr. Scott – they certainly were for her – and that Mrs. Scott was not yet emotionally able to talk about him. In the beginning, they spoke almost exclusively about Adie, but as time passed and mutual trust grew, they began to talk about themselves and each other. One afternoon Mr. Scott surprised her by saying, "I have devised a survival plan. I'm going to revel in my experience as Adie's father," he said. "My twenty years with him was the highlight of my life. So, I'm going to appreciate what a gift he was, instead of dwelling on how empty life will be without him. What do you think?"

"I think it's a wonderful approach. The question is: can you do it?"

"Of course I can. Know why? Because it's true. Having him in our life *was* a blessing!" Nellie was skeptical, but she wondered if she might apply his solution to the anger and loneliness she felt not only from Adie's death, but also from the loss of her father. He had drowned in a sailing accident when she was sixteen. *Next time I resent losing my men or can't sleep because I miss them so much,* she thought, *I'll try Mr. Scott's solution. It might help.*

By mid-winter, Nellie was becoming curious about Mrs. Scott because she never saw her during her Sunday morning visits. She always inquired about her out of courtesy, but Mr. Scott's answers were not particularly informative. Then, one cold Sunday morning Mr. Scott said, "Would you like to walk this morning, rather than sit in the kitchen?"

"Sure," she replied, suspecting Mr. Scott had a reason for his proposal.

They walked without speaking for a block or two until Mr. Scott got to the point. "Jane's not getting better, Nell. She has flashes of anger, crying jags and refuses to see a doctor. I say things that upset her, but I don't know why they upset her. I just don't know how to talk to her anymore." After a brief pause, as if he were considering his options one last time, he said, "This is your field, Nell. What do you think?"

Nellie knew a good deal about loss and grief because she had faced the challenge of her mother's decline after her father's death. She had spent hours with Helen Holden, a psychiatric nurse at the hospital and an old friend of her mother, discussing what to do and what not to do to help her regain her health. It had been a long road, but Lottie was up and running again and gave much credit to her oldest daughter for her rehabilitation.

"Your wife needs professional help," Nellie began, "but your job is to convince her that you understand how she feels. If you can do that she won't feel so alone and she'll begin to think the way she feels is normal, given the circumstances."

"But how do I convince her?"

"By saying things to her like: 'You must feel crushed by this loss, Jane;' or, 'a mother can't suffer a worse loss than you have.' I know these sentiments sound trite and obvious, but that's what she needs to hear. She needs to know she is not the only one who feels devastated." Although they discussed Nellie's advice for some time, Nellie was not sure Mr. Scott accepted it. He was giving it

155

serious thought though. The vertical creases between his eyebrows told her so.

"By the way, how are you holding up?" Nellie asked. "How's your survival plan working?"

"I miss him, of course. I have a permanent ache inside, but honestly, I'm so grateful he was a part of our lives, that we enjoyed each other so much. I also feel good when I think of him." Nellie was impressed. She had tried Mr. Scott's antidote, but it did not seem to help her sleep when she awoke in the wee hours thinking of Adie.

This happened often. She could fall asleep because she was exhausted, but slept fitfully and awoke after only two or three hours. The early morning hours were torture. She relived every moment, every conversation, every laugh they had had. The lack of sleep and the sadness made her tired and she could feel the clutches of depression grasping at her.

Mr. Scott called only one week later. "When do you graduate?" he asked without preamble.

"Five weeks from today," she said. "Will you come to the ceremony?"

"I need to talk to you in person," he said. "Could you drop by sometime?"

At eight o'clock the next evening, she was on her way to the Scotts'. One year had passed since Spencer had learned of Adie's death. *So far, 1918 has been filled with rubble from Adie's death!* Nellie thought. *Heartache, guilt, loneliness... The only positive thing that's come of it is my conversations with Mr. Scott. Thank goodness for him.*

~~~

Mr. Scott answered the doorbell dressed in corduroy pants, a shapeless red sweater, and woolen socks. He apologized for his looks while running his fingers through his uncombed hair. Nellie shook his outstretched hand and said, "Your hair looks as if Adie had just run by and mussed it." Nellie knew he loved remembering little things like that.

"If only he had," he answered, leading the way to the kitchen.

"So, what's on your mind?" she asked. "Your voice sounded urgent last night."

"I am nervous about this actually. I have a favor to ask of you ... more of an idea really ... or a proposal for you to consider."

"Just say it. That's the best way."

"Okay." He leaned forward and said, "After you graduate, I would like to hire you to take care of Jane."

"Me? Why me?"

"Because no one is better qualified," he said seriously. "You know the patient and her problems, her doctor, her history, and her husband. It would take a more experienced nurse several months to acquire the knowledge you already have. Plus you have experience with grief, having lost your father and helped your mother recover from her loss." Nellie was fascinated by the way he delivered his pitch. He never took his eyes off hers.

"I don't care to talk about salary with you because I could never look upon you as an employee, but I promise I will pay you well. If you're interested, we can talk about that later." He stopped, exhaled, and said, "So, what do you think? Tell me. I'm still nervous."

"The sales pitch was excellent, but you didn't need it. Of course I will do it, but there is a potential problem. A year ago, after I came here to express my condolences, there was talk around town about you and me. It was all over school. Did you know that?"

"Yes, I heard about those insinuations from my plant manager," Mr. Scott said, "but I couldn't figure how that stuff got started. How did it? Do you know?"

"We kissed and I remember holding your hands when I said goodbye. Some folks saw that and they're envious," Nellie said.

"Of what?" he asked.

"Of you," Nellie replied. "You have a reputation in Spencer as a smart, wealthy entrepreneur. Therefore, some folks around town envy you, or even dislike you. That's why, when they heard you were kissing a woman half your age the day your son died, they had scandalous thoughts." She let this caricature sink in before adding, "I'm sure you and I can handle the lies, but I'm thinking of my patient now, your wife. She's fragile. These rumors have the potential of hurting her."

"You're right, they do and you should be thinking about her first, Nell. That's why I hope you'll take this job. And about the rumors: I don't know if Jane's heard them, but I'll ask her."

"No, let me do that," Nellie said. "We girls have to confront this together because if she has any doubts about my motives or loyalty to her, we won't be able to accomplish anything and you'll have to find someone else."

One week after graduation, Nellie began work as nurse-companion to Mrs. Scott. Over tea in Jane's

bedroom, the two fell into a catty conversation about Spencer's mayor who had been photographed in New York with a burlesque dancer. Nellie was slightly embarrassed to be giggling over the man's misadventure until she realized she might turn their conversation toward last year's rumors of her relationship with Mr. Scott.

"You know, Mrs. Scott," she began cautiously, "*I* was the subject of some slanderous talk a year ago. I wanted to …"

"Shhh," Mrs. Scott said, placing an index finger on her lips. "I know what has been said about you and my husband. My friends keep me current."

"Yes, but let me assure you that …"

"No need, my dear, no need," Mrs. Scott said. Nellie heard the unspoken words *discussion over*, repeated for emphasis, but she could not acquiesce. If she permitted her patient, an older and more experienced woman, to dismiss this conversation, she would be conceding to her the prerogative of dismissing other important conversations in the future. So, she moved her chair forward, took Mrs. Scott's two hands in hers, and said, "I can help you overcome your loss, Mrs. Scott, but only if you trust me. I admire your husband, but I am not in love with him. If you have any doubts about this, you and he should find someone else to help you." Nellie stopped there, but continued to hold Mrs. Scott's hands and to look her in the eye.

"I would like you to continue coming, Miss Knight. I am willing to see if this will help."

"The question is: do you trust me?" Nellie persisted. A long pause ensued. Nellie held her tongue. Silence was a tactic that often seemed to oblige patients to respond.

"I have never had even the slightest reason to believe my husband has a wandering eye," she said finally, but I've been a poor wife since Adie..." she could not finish the sentence. "But no, I believe you. I do."

"Thank you." Nellie said before letting go of Mrs. Scott's hands.

The next morning, while Mr. Scott was preparing his wife's breakfast – his usual routine – Nellie told him the "scandal issue" had been resolved.

"Yes," he replied. "Jane told me last night at dinner and, by the way, she was impressed by the way you handled it, which doesn't happen often, believe me."

With that exchange, collaboration was born. It began with Mrs. Scott routinely recapping at dinner the conversations she had had with Nellie during the day. She admitted to her husband that she talked about Adie incessantly with Nellie. "I cry half the time I'm with her; the other half she's about to cry." In turn, Mr. Scott began to inform Nellie of his wife's reactions to issues the two women had discussed the previous day. There was a hint of subterfuge in this arrangement. The husband's betrayals of his wife's confidences bothered Nellie, but she let it continue because it was so useful. Mrs. Scott was not easy to read; she kept her feelings to herself. Mr. Scott's insights reduced the chances of misunderstandings and warned Nellie of issues to be addressed with extra care. In addition, Nellie was pleased Mr. Scott had found a useful

role to play. It was comforting to know she had a partner in this complex undertaking.

For the first months of Nellie's employment, Mrs. Scott was always in bed no matter what time Nellie arrived. Invariably, she would greet Nellie with an apology and an excuse about being tired, after which she would get up, put on her robe, offer Nellie tea or coffee, and comment on the weather. These were ingrained, learned courtesies; she went through them by rote, never varying the order or wording of her routine. Mrs. Scott was functioning on a semi-conscious level.

As 1919 rolled in, Nellie was also concerned with Mrs. Scott's weight loss. The family doctor, Malcolm O'Hagan, looked for causes and found nothing specific. He attributed her loss to decreased calorie intake and a generally fragile constitution. Fortunately, Mrs. Scott's beauty was not disappearing with the pounds. Her fair skin, still flawless, her almond-shaped hazel eyes, made larger by her gaunt face, and her thick reddish brown hair, made a stunning combination. Rumor had it that since adolescence she had stopped men in their tracks and left envious women in her wake. Nellie found it encouraging that Mrs. Scott still took pride in her appearance, and yet there were signs the depression was taking its toll. She moved slowly and her wan smile reflected neither happiness nor amusement, but rather acceptance of her state. Nellie guessed that Mrs. Scott had not noticed life's lighter side since Adie died almost two years ago.

In fact, she had not ventured out of her house for months. She lived in her bedroom, which felt subterranean to Nellie. Dark damask fabric covered the walls, drapes

were drawn against the light of day – so Mrs. Scott could sleep anytime – and a thick carpet insulated the room from outside noise. The massive mahogany posts of her canopied bed loomed like dark pallbearers in the anemic light of two lamps. *The poor thing is living in her own mausoleum,* Nellie thought. She could not help imagining darkness closing in on her patient, rolling over her like a poisonous mist as she lay alone in that big bed. Nellie wondered if she had taken on more than she could handle.

One day in early spring, around noon there was a knock at the bedroom door and Mr. Scott entered. He was home for lunch, wearing a tan suit and a boater in acknowledgment of spring's arrival. With a spring in his step, he headed straight for his wife. He gave her a kiss and a bouquet of flowers. Then he took off his hat, held it over his heart, and sang a few bars of <u>Pack Up Your Troubles in Your Old Kit Bag.</u> His presence lifted the gloom. Nellie left to give them time alone. As she closed the door, she saw them both leaning forward in conversation. *She's sad and angry and tired much of the time and yet he adores her. That must be love,* she thought with a touch of envy.

As spring bloomed and Nellie saw little improvement in her patient, she scheduled a meeting with her mentor, Helen Holden. Helen was not discouraged. "Be patient," she advised. "So long as she continues to be willing to talk about Adie, she's keeping the door open."

Nellie took heart shortly thereafter. Something she said about Adie's coloring propelled Mrs. Scott into a fifteen-minute monologue about how handsome he was.

"He had a two-page spread modeling clothes in Photoplay Magazine when he was six," she bragged.

"I'd love to see those pictures," Nellie said, "if you still have the magazine."

"I do have that magazine, but it hurts me to look at it. I should think it would hurt you too," Mrs. Scott said caustically.

"Sometimes it does, but I'm trying to fill my memory with every picture and piece of information I can find."

"Why would you do that, for goodness sake?" Mrs. Scott shot back.

"Because," Nellie hesitated, "after I lost my father I forgot what he looked like. It was awful because it made me feel that I didn't love him enough to remember him." Mrs. Scott was quiet.

Several minutes later she said, "I could never forget what Adie looked like. Never!"

"Of course you couldn't. You were his mother. You suffered an incomparable loss. But, I lost my first love. I've never told you this, but I hoped to marry Adie a few years down the road. Do you know when I fell for him?"

"No, tell me." Mrs. Scott was instantly interested.

"Last year, we started to walk home after school and Adie spotted three big kids picking on John Burdick behind the school. One shoved him so hard he fell down. John's a little strange and is picked on often, but Adie ran down there and stopped them from beating him up. As the two of them walked back up the hill to where I was waiting, Adie had his hand on John's shoulder. They stopped and Adie said, 'Nellie, this is my friend John.'

That's when I fell for him." Nellie stopped, almost overcome with emotion. Jane patted the back of her hand.

"My dear," she said.

The next morning, while Mr. Scott was preparing his wife's breakfast, he said, "Jane was upset by your conversation yesterday."

"I know. I'm sorry, but we were on target. That'll happen."

"She was upset because she thought she upset you."

"Well, that's interesting. If you're right, that's a significant change because up to now her focus has been exclusively on herself. We'll see."

Two weeks later as Nellie was leaving, Mrs. Scott said, "We have quite a slew of unsorted photographs in the attic. You're welcome to look through them if you wish."

"I'd love to," Nellie answered. "And I'll let you know how it goes. I'll be your canary in the mine shaft."

At ten o'clock that evening, Nellie carried a large cardboard box of photos into her room and dumped them on her bed. Although she intended to spend only an hour looking through them, she was hooked from the very first picture and felt drawn irresistibly to look at the next one and the next. Nellie shed her first tear when she saw a picture of Adie, at two weeks of age, serene in his organdy christening dress. Another ran down her cheek when she saw a little boy standing straight and proud on a dock holding a three inch sunfish. Their prom photo, on the other hand, taken in front of a fake forest backdrop, made them look like Madame Tussaud's wax mannequins, but it did evoke wonderful memories – and more tears. She sorted through yellowing pictures curled at the corners,

newspaper photos documenting Adie's baseball exploits, formal portraits, and candid snapshots. Around 4 a.m., she looked at the last picture and fell asleep with cheeks still moist and memories of Adie on all sides of her.

The next morning she returned the pictures. Mrs. Scott looked at her and asked, "So, what does the canary have to report?"

"It was very emotional, but I loved being with him and I thank you for letting me see them." Mrs. Scott just nodded, and Nellie could see anxiety in her eyes.

A month passed before Mr. Scott reported a minor victory. "We looked at photos last night and we both cried. I don't know if she'll want to look at more, but she could never have done that six months ago."

This step forward occurred as Spencer's long awaited spring began to show its colors. Nellie brought Mrs. Scott a bouquet of daffodils when she noticed her opening the curtains most mornings to observe the renewal process was in full bloom in her backyard. "I haven't done anything about my garden flowers," she said to no one.

"There's still time," Nellie suggested.

"Yes, there is," she said. "Soon enough I'll be ready, I think."

"Timing's the key," Mr. Scott told Nellie later. "It's like landing a big fish. When she's fighting you, don't try to reel her in. Reel her in when she's tired from fighting you." So, Nellie waited and when the daffodils began to wither, she brought her stargazer lilies, Mrs. Scott's very favorite, and by late May, the two women were at work tilling, composting, and planting several flats of Mrs. Scott's other favorites: sweet alyssum, heliotrope, and portulaca.

Mrs. Scott tired easily from the gardening, but the exercise, fresh air, and plants lifted her spirits and Nellie sensed progress. Mrs. Scott, who lived in France until she was twenty-three, had promised to help Nellie with her French when she regained her energy. The day they began work in the garden, Mrs. Scott, true to her word, reminded Nellie of her offer. So it was agreed: they would speak only French in the garden. Mr. Scott worked with the women on weekends but had little aptitude for languages. Not to be outdone, he appeared one Sunday morning with a beret on his head, a cigarette holder in his mouth, and a pencil-thin mustache drawn on his upper lip with burned cork. When he spoke, it was in English but with a heavy French accent. The props, the mustache, and the accent created such a silly image that Mrs. Scott laughed aloud. At that moment, Nellie caught Mr. Scott's eye and gave a subtle nod of approval. He understood the gesture and smiled affectionately at her. *The 'rare bird' is a cute guy,* she thought, *even with that fake mustache.*

Her memories of those stolen glances visited her frequently during the days that followed. They interrupted her when she was busy and haunted her during quiet moments. A week later, a disjointed version of those memories appeared in her dreams and awakened her in the middle of the night. Wide-awake, Nellie made a cup of hot tea and climbed back in bed, not to sleep, but to take stock. *What exactly is happening here?*

Why was he in her dreams? They had worked together for almost two years and this had not happened before. They had grown close sharing thoughts in long discussions about life and how to reintegrate Mrs. Scott into it. As she

thought back over their talks and times, she realized they had discussed just about everything except their own relationship. *Understandable,* she thought. *My attention was on Mrs. Scott. My relationship with Mr. Scott was not the issue.* However, Nellie had just made it the issue. She was questioning an unspoken agreement they had which bound them to silence on various personal matters and forbade them to touch. To Nellie's recollection, they had not been in physical contact since day they learned of Adie's death. Why not? She had no romantic designs on Mr. Scott and he had been the perfect gentleman.

But things are changing. Nellie could sense it and the circumstances – she hesitated to acknowledge – were permissive, to say the least. One vulnerable man feeling over the hill and alone. One attractive, young woman feeling sympathy and admiration for that man. The two working together in an emotional environment. Put them in the Scotts' backyard, add spring, laughter, and French conversation. The result: transformation, a joint effort becomes a partnership, then a relationship . . . Nellie felt a chill as she saw where this was headed. She pulled the blanket up over her shoulders and sipped her warm tea. *Okay, maybe I do have feelings for him,* she admitted reluctantly. *The question is, what am I to do with them?*

She felt her face flush. "Damn!" she said aloud, but quietly. She had been betrayed. This had happened without her knowledge or approval. Worse yet, it was hopeless. *He may well be the man for me, but the dream is too far-fetched to ever come true.* She went to the bathroom, splashed water on her face, and watched the drops run off her chin and down the drain. *Right down the*

drain, she thought. She padded back to bed, going over her conclusions, hoping to find a flaw in her thinking that, if changed, would produce a more welcome outcome, but that did not happen. Finally, as the first hint of dawn touched the sky, she breathed a deep sigh and closed her eyes. *Maybe it is better to know the truth than be surprised by it,* she thought as she nodded off to sleep, sitting up, cold teacup in hand.

The next morning as she prepared to go to work, her mind fastened on the question of resignation. Ethically she thought she should, but wouldn't it be unethical if her resignation delayed or derailed Mrs. Scott's recovery and how would she explain her reason for resigning? Despite all her concerns, she was happy to be going to the Scotts' that morning. She looked forward to seeing Mr. Scott, to hearing his voice, his reasoning and his reasonableness in their morning strategy session. But, when she walked into the kitchen, Mrs. Scott was there making her husband's breakfast, a reversal of roles. Nellie's face must have registered surprise because Mrs. Scott shrugged and said, "I felt like getting up and being useful." As if to prove it, she poured Nellie a cup of coffee and as she handed it to her she asked, "Are you alright? You look tired."

"I'm okay," she said. "Just woke up too early this morning and couldn't go back to sleep."

Mrs. Scott reached out and offered Nellie her hand. "We have our good days and bad days and often we don't know why, right? We just have to trust that as time goes by we'll have more good days than bad." This was the new Jane Scott. Still holding Nellie's hand she said, "I think of us as sisters in grief, Nellie. People who haven't lost a

loved one just can't appreciate the depth of our pain. It's impossible"

Nellie was touched. Mrs. Scott gave her a brief hug and whispered, "Thank you, my dear." Her behavior and her eyes told Nellie that she was on the road to recovery; she was no longer isolated from the world by her misfortune. It would take time but perhaps she already had an inkling that the gloom that had dominated her thoughts, the pictures of her son's crash that had played and replayed in her head, the insomnia and the fatigue – were beginning to lift.

Nellie was happy for the Scotts, of course, and as the person most involved in helping Mrs. Scott find her way back, she should have been dancing gleefully around the kitchen table as Adie had done so long ago. But her heart was heavy, she was numb from fatigue, and she was laboring to keep her emotions in check. She fetched a molasses cookie from the jar and sat down heavily at the kitchen table. Mr. Scott came in dressed for work, greeted the women, and sat down across from Nellie. They exchanged glances, but no words. Again, words were not necessary. Nellie knew the curtain on this play was coming down and unless she had badly misjudged Mr. Scott, so did he.

~~~

Children dressed for the brisk autumn mornings, marched noisily to school, shuffling through the orange and yellow leaves. Adie had been gone more than two years when the Village Council voted to name a park for him. During the dedication ceremony, the high school band played a medley of John Philip Sousa marches and

concluded with *God Bless America.* The mayor spoke, and Mr. Scott delivered a two-minute thank you speech, after which he glanced down at his wife, who was sitting next to him. To his surprise, Mrs. Scott stood, stepped toward the microphone and said, "I was so proud of my Adie for so many reasons. Today I am equally proud of this town, of all of you, for recognizing him in this way. Thank you so much." The park was full that sunny September afternoon. Most of those present knew of Mrs. Scott's long struggle to recover from her son's death and the applause for her lasted some time.

Mrs. Scott returned to her seat but rose twice and smiled, acknowledging the applause. Then Mr. Scott rose to stand with her for a final bow, but she could not get up. Seeing her difficulty, the crowd finally stopped clapping as Dr. Malcolm O'Hagan, the Scotts' family doctor, climbed onto the dais and felt her forehead.

"Home and to bed," he said in his strong Irish brogue. "I will be there forthwith." Upon examination, Dr. O'Hagan found his patient had a high fever, a bright red throat, and achiness in her joints. He diagnosed her with a strep throat infection and ordered the usual: aspirin, gargles, and cool compresses. Then, to relieve her anxiety he said, "Jane, you are in good company. Ten percent of Spencer has the same thing." But, he was worried. Even before Adie's death, Mrs. Scott had not been a strong woman and since his death, her depression had undermined her health. She had eaten and slept poorly, lost weight, and even lost interest in life briefly. "I'll be back first thing in the morning," Dr. O'Hagan said, holding her hand.

Mr. Scott and Nellie accompanied the doctor to the door. "Goodbye, my friends," he said, but as he turned away, Nellie put her hand on his arm and pulled him back so he was facing them.

"What do you think?" she asked.

"I don't care to speculate now," he said firmly.

"Malcolm," Mr. Scott said, and paused until the doctor had turned and was looking at him. Still, he delayed a beat or two, holding the doctor's attention with his presence. Finally, he asked, "How worried are you?"

Dr. O'Hagan was not known for his bedside manner but he did have keen political instincts and they were picking up the scent of impatience from a powerful man who expected more information than he had been given.

"Charles, your Janie has a high fever, probably from a bacterial infection. We need her immune system to fight for her now, but we both know she has not been a robust creature since she lost her son. I need time to assess the seriousness of this infection and her response to it. I'll be at home this evening and you may call me any time for any reason." He closed the door behind him, leaving Mr. Scott and Nellie in the vestibule looking at each other.

Without a word, Nellie once again stepped forward into the tall man's embrace. The human contact was comforting. Moved by it and feeling immeasurably sad, Nellie almost cried. *Not now*, she ordered; *stay strong for Charles.* After several seconds, she backed out of his arms and said, "Your speech was perfect this afternoon. I was proud of you."

Come have a molasses cookie," he said. They sat at the kitchen table, which held so many happy memories, but

this time there was no light banter. The doctor's warning had frightened them. Nellie knew that streptococcus infections could lead to scarlet fever, a cruel "flesh eating" disease that had taken thousands lives in the 19th century. Neither mentioned contagion or quarantine, but they knew they had already been exposed and that at – or even before – the first sign of scarlet fever, a notice would have to be posted on the Scotts' front door. Nellie suggested she move into the guest bedroom to be available at any hour and Mr. Scott nodded his agreement. As they tidied the kitchen, he looked down at her and said, "I'm sorry to have roped you into this."

"I'm happy to be here...with you, Charles," Nellie replied. It was the first time she had called him by his Christian name. It sounded warmer to her than C.K., which most of his friends called him. He reached out, took her hand, and squeezed it. "That sounds good," he said.

Before going to bed, Nellie checked on Mrs. Scott. She took her temperature, encouraged her to drink some tea, sponged her off with a cool compress, and asked her if anything hurt. Mrs. Scott shook her head. Nellie put a small bell on her bedside table and told her to ring it if she needed anything. She sat by the bed and held Mrs. Scott's hand until she fell asleep.

For the next few days, her symptoms diminished. Dr. O'Hagan visited daily, watched her temperature drop, her sore throat subside, and her energy begin to return. "This is how a strep infection normally runs its course," he told C.K. truthfully. "Nonetheless, let's just keep our fingers crossed for another week or two."

One week passed slowly. On the ninth day, Mrs. Scott got out of bed and worked in her garden for an hour. C.K. noticed other positive signs during that week: a smile graced her lips two or three times and he himself made a light-hearted remark to Dr. O'Hagan. But the doctor was characteristically serious. The threat of scarlet fever was still real and there was nothing they could do, other than watch, wait, and hope.

On the morning of the fifteenth day, Mrs. Scott awoke with joint pain and a low-grade fever. Nellie called Dr. O'Hagan who came to the Scott home immediately. His exam produced one more worrisome symptom: a drop in blood pressure. His medical responsibility required him to hang an official quarantine sign on the Scotts' front door, which he did reluctantly. In his years of practice, he had seen patients and families give up when that sign was posted. It was as if it kept away not only friends and neighbors, but also the will to live.

During her final days, an itchy rash on her neck and face finally robbed Jane Scott of her beauty. Knowing how upset she would be if she saw herself, Nellie and C.K. kept mirrors from her by washing her face and brushing her hair themselves. At the very end, she was confused and then incoherent, which made it impossible for them to know if she heard them say their goodbyes. A memorial service, attended by more than two-hundred friends, was held for her at St. Mark's Episcopal Church on Main Street, after which Jane was laid to rest in the town cemetery.

~~~

C.K. gave Nellie an excessively generous severance check and thanked her for all she had done, but to Nellie his farewell seemed stilted. There was no embrace, no expressed hope they would stay in touch, no mention of the respect and affection he had for her. In fact, he broke off their farewell by saying, "I hope you'll excuse me, my lawyer is waiting for me with a stack of papers to be signed."

"Yes, of course," she said sounding as perfunctory as he had. She walked home with the sadness of having lost a friend and patient and the emptiness of having been dismissed by the one she loved. Lottie must have seen the hurt in her eyes when she opened the door. She took her daughter in her arms and for the first time Nellie's tears flowed.

Nellie was an independent, confident, good-looking young woman when Mrs. Scott died. She had a profession, respect, and many friends and acquaintances, but for the next few months, she felt isolated and deserted. She no longer had access to the man of her dreams and so far, she had not been able to find a way to reestablish it. She did find motivation to continue trying, however. It came from a doctor with whom Nellie was making rounds. He urged his students to anticipate their patients' needs and take the initiative in treating them. "Remember," he said, "Better to do something than to do nothing." *He's right,* she thought. *This is a tall order, but I've got to do something. I've got to try.*

Her first obstacle was the mourning etiquette, which dictated that a widower be given a full year and privacy to mourn his loss, contemplate life, and accommodate public

expectations. But for Nellie, a year loomed like an eternity. She saw time and separation as her enemies and feared they could loosen the bonds she and C.K. had forged at such a terrible cost. The trick would be to reestablish contact with him naturally, without intruding on his grieving period. If she could just talk with him, perhaps they could arrange a way to stay in touch privately.

Nellie's first decision was to keep a respectful distance from him for at least three months. During that time, she wrote him a thank-you note for the generous bonus he had given her in hopes that he would respond, but he did not. She walked past his house on her way to and from work, but their paths never crossed. Time passed without contact and Nellie advised herself to be patient. *Luck or Fate will intercede.*

Her second decision was to tell C.K. how she felt the next time she saw him. If she did not, she feared that many months might pass before she would have another opportunity, and anything could happen in the interim. In the meantime, because she had no one to talk with, she held conversations with her father. She imagined he would say, "Your mother seemed to admire C.K. She will stick with you, but keep your own counsel, Honey. This is too juicy to share." Three days before Christmas, that proved to be wise advice.

The day was grey and so bitterly cold it felt as if the air itself had frozen. At dawn, snow began to fall, big flakes dropping straight down in the still air. For hours, they piled up, silently softening every angle, decorating each cupola and stoop, blanketing every shrub, berry, and blade. Walking home that evening, Nellie was awed by the

strength and delicacy of the village's big trees. Maples, oaks, and sycamores stood like sentinels on both sides of the streets and formed arches high above. Looking up, she could see that even the slightest branches were laden with enough snow to be definable against the black sky. At six o'clock, as she turned right onto Grant Avenue, the street lamps came on, illuminating the falling flakes and warming the wintery scene with their buttery light. At the other end of the street a man, diminutive under the towering trees, turned left onto Grant and hunched his shoulders against the cold. Nellie recognized his lanky silhouette. The moment had arrived. She could feel the excitement increase as the distance between them diminished.

"My dear Nell, what a coincidence. I was just thinking about you," he said, extending his gloved hand.

"Merry Christmas, Charles. I was thinking of you too and here we are right in front of your house." Nellie took his hand.

"Yes, so we are, and since we're here, would you have time to come in for a molasses cookie?"

"Even if I were going to the White House tonight, I'd make time to have a molasses cookie with you." C.K. held her hand as they made their way up the unshoveled walk and across the front porch.

Inside, C.K. excused himself and ran upstairs. He was back immediately with two wool sweaters and two pairs of wool socks. "The house gets chilly during the day," he said handing Nellie one of each. "No one should be uncomfortable while eating cookies."

"Tell me how you are. I've worried about you," Nellie said, pulling the sweater over her head. She was not cold, but she felt herself shaking. He stood at the end of the long kitchen table and answered her thoughtfully. "In a nutshell," he concluded, "I am well, but I'm lonely too." When he finished, he retrieved the cookie jar and the milk pitcher and draped himself into a chair across the table from Nellie. She seized the moment.

"I have something to say to you, Charles, and I'd ask you to listen only, okay? No comments until I am finished."

"Agreed," he said.

She reached across the table and took one of his hands in both of hers. She focused her blue-gray eyes on his eyes and said quietly, "I love you, Charles. I'm in love with you. I want to spend my life with you." He started to respond, but she raised her hand, palm toward him, like a traffic cop, and continued. "I've known you for several years and seen you under the most trying circumstances a father and a husband can endure. I can't imagine anyone bearing up under such tragedies with more strength and grace than you have. I know we could set off one hellacious scandal in Spencer, but I don't give a hoot about that and I don't care that you are twice my age. For centuries, couples with age differences greater than ours have been happy. Only one thing could persuade me that this is a bad idea, and that's if you tell me you don't love me."

Nellie released his hand. He withdrew it and studied his fingernails. He sat absolutely still for what seemed like an eternity to Nellie. When he looked up, he swallowed hard and wiped a tear from his eye.

"I am flattered beyond words, Nell. I must admit I've intentionally not made contact with you since Jane's service because...well, I was afraid to face the facts. You are braver than I am and a remarkable woman, but do you have any idea what this would do to your mother?"

"Yes, I do. Mother will be uncomfortable because it will raise eyebrows and she dislikes controversy. But when I tell her I love you, she'll support me...and," she added as an afterthought, "I'll support her. We have faced tough times together before. Besides, she will grow to love you herself. How could she not?"

They talked into the evening. They agreed there would be a divide in town and that those who would oppose them would make the most noise. They touched on the idea that they might have to leave Spencer if the reaction were too strong and Nellie asked how this would affect C.K.'s business. They weighed options and assessed possibilities. *It's not me versus him in this conversation,* Nellie realized. *It's us against various challengers.* Nellie was encouraged by this, but she sensed hesitation on his part still.

When they were full of cookies and empty of new ideas, a brief silence descended. An occasional creak from the old house standing against the frigid night and the tick-tock of the kitchen clock were the only sounds they heard. Nellie glanced at the clock.

"Do you have to go?" C. K. asked. "Do you have a commitment?"

"I'm not leaving until you tell me what's bothering you," Nellie said. "I've seen that look on your wonderful

face before and it tells me you're unhappy about something."

"Frankly, I'm concerned about the difference in our ages, Nell," C.K. blurted out. "All too soon I'm going to be an old man, and you'll still be a young woman. I. . ."

Nellie's response interrupted Mr. Scott and hit hard. "I would give a lifetime for five years with you," she whispered in a shaky voice.

It brought silence back to the room. Nellie lowered her eyes and C.K. sighed deeply, exhaling the tension that had been building since they had met on the sidewalk.

"Okay," he said, throwing up his hands and grinning broadly. "Okay, you've got me. And let me tell you something else: you've had me for a long time."

Epilogue

Nellie Scott, 95 years old, sat looking out the bay window of her comfortable living room. She was watching the kids shuffle through the orange and yellow leaves on their way home from school. She never tired of the scene. She recalled being a part of it long ago, skipping home with her playmates while avoiding the cracks in the sidewalk and, later, strolling home with Adie, in love for the first time.

Although Nellie had never been one to reminisce, as age imposed limitations on her body, memories became a diversion from boredom. They flew at her like birds in the night, unseen and unbidden. Adie appeared often. Even as she approached the century mark, Nellie mourned his loss. She mourned C.K. too and the life they could have had,

especially since she was given only three of the five years she had promised "would be worth a lifetime". C.K. had died in their bed on Christmas Eve in 1925 at 55 years of age. *Ah, but it was a joy while it lasted,* Nellie recalled. They had honeymooned aboard a sailboat in the Caribbean, traveled to New York and Paris, produced a healthy son, and C.K. had sold his business for a small fortune. Memories of the bitter public discussion of the propriety of their marriage came home to roost too. The couple had chosen a life together and knew it was the right decision, but they had paid a price: Nellie had lost her job and both had lost friends, Dr. O'Hagan among them. Nonetheless, by the time of C.K's death, the winds of scandal had blown themselves out and most news agencies wrote admiringly of his accomplishments and philanthropies. *The New York Times* obituary did not even mention the scandal.

The parade of students had ended. The afternoon shadows had lengthened and then disappeared in the dusk. Around ten o'clock Nellie had a glass of milk and a molasses cookie, as was her custom, and climbed into bed for a long sleep.

THE UMP

When I was twelve years old, my stepfather, who was a sergeant in the Army, interrupted my breakfast on my first day of summer vacation. "We're moving to Germany in a couple months, Kid," he said, "so you better put all that baseball shit behind you, you hear? They don't have the vaguest idea what baseball is in Germany." I promise you those were his words verbatim. I'll never forget them. Exactly sixty years have passed since that morning. I know because DiMaggio was married that same year, 1954.

I remember just about everything about that morning. I was sitting at the wobbly, Formica-topped card table in our kitchen, eating Cheerios with no milk, the radio was on as usual, and my mother had already gone to school to finish paperwork. It was a hot, still Georgia morning and we had no air conditioning in our trailer. When my stepfather delivered his message, he stood close and hovered above me so the rancid-sweet smells of his sweat and Aqua Velva after-shave lotion stayed in my nostrils for hours. He wore no shirt because he liked to show off his muscles. They were pretty impressive, actually, because he pumped iron in the driveway every night. He stood there looking down at me for five or ten seconds and then suddenly yelled "BOO!" at the top of his lungs. It scared me silly. He pulled stunts like that all the time.

His news almost made me throw up. Our transfer, if it occurred, would keep me from doing something I did

really well; it would force me to say goodbye to our coach, who was a great guy; and probably it would mean I would never again play in front of many spectators. Most importantly, it would deprive my mother of her greatest pleasure – watching me play. She knew baseball inside and out, having learned it from my real father, who had been a famous player in Cuba. I had to do something; I could not give this man the pleasure of taking away such an important part of my life.

I'm telling you right now, LEE Roy, I said, accenting the first word of his double name because he hated it pronounced that way. I'm playing this season. I'm playing the whole damned season, one way, or the other.

You'll do exactly as I tell ya to do, or you'll suffer the consequences, he yelled at me as I ran out the door.

Several days later, without telling my mother or LEE Roy, I called my Granny to ask if she could help somehow. She lived in Savannah, had money, and a big soft spot for me. After thinking it over and asking some questions, she said, If your mother agrees, I'll call leROY – accent on the second name – and tell him you and I will find a little place to rent until your games are finished. Then I'll fly to Germany with you. We can make a fun trip of it. I was hopeful LEE Roy would accept this plan because it wouldn't cost him anything; my mother would be with him all the time, plus he'd get rid of me for a month or more. Besides, he was ignoring my mother's suggestion that she stay home with me and join him in Germany as soon as my season ended.

I did play that season – before we left. It was only for a few weeks, but they were the best weeks of my Little

League career. I hit five home runs in five consecutive games and batted .406. My hopes of playing all season began to fade, though, one night when I heard my stepfather on the phone speaking in an impatient tone to my Granny. You ain't gonna fly with him to Germany, he said. That ain't your job, it's mine or his mother's, but it sure ain't yours. The next morning I overheard him cussing at my mother for siding with her mother, not with him. My heart sank.

It almost broke a week later. LEE Roy came home from happy hour with a snoot full. He took his shirt off and put his foot down – hard. In a slightly slurred, obscenity-filled rant, he said that his family was not a goddamned democracy. We don't discuss things till we're blue in the face, he said. And we sure as hell don't vote on things. You do what you're told and I'm telling you loud and clear, we *are* going to Germany as a goddamned family. And we did. Neither my mother nor Granny thought it wise to push him further.

Of course, they knew that Germany was not the real problem. As it turned out, our apartment and my school were considerably better there than in Georgia. LEE Roy and I were the problem and it was getting worse. I started smoking and I burned myself on purpose in front of other kids to show them how tough I was. My grades were poor and I refused to speak to LEE Roy – about anything. I was developing a real hatred of the man and believed with good reason that he hated me. Then we hit rock bottom.

My *Sport Magazine*, the *Sports Illustrated* of its day, arrived in the mail one afternoon. I took it to my room, lay on my bed, and began to read it carefully, front to back. In

183

mid-magazine, I flipped the page and I think my heart stopped. I remember my vision dimmed for an instant. All I could see was reddish-black. When it returned, I was looking at an article on the Little League World Series in which my team was prominently featured. There was a picture of Tommy Taylor, my best friend, lining a double to center field and another of the group, my gang, standing and kneeling in front of a dark green dugout with their arms around each other. Even now, as an old man, who has been through illness, the loss of a child, and a divorce, it hurts to think of missing that World Series.

When I did not come down for dinner, my stepfather came up to get me. He saw the expression on my face and the article open on my bed and figured it out. Don't look so down in the dumps, Kid, he said, you wouldn't have played well at that level anyway. The pressure would be too much for you. Then he looked at me and began to laugh. He continued laughing as strutted out of my room and started down the stairs. I raced through the bedroom doorway and I launched myself at him feet first like I was doing the long jump. He was turning as my feet struck his upper arm and neck. That's the last thing I remember until I became aware that I was lying on the sofa with a buzzing sound in my left ear, a bad cut over my left eye, and my mother looking down at me. Her hair was mussed, her blouse was ripped, and she looked as if she were in pain. LEE Roy was nowhere to be seen and I did not dare ask where he was.

Mother called the hospital, reported that she and I were injured, and needed attention. During our ambulance ride to the infirmary, I overheard her telling one of the corpsmen that her husband hit me with his fist when we

landed at the bottom of the stairs and then hit her as she attempted to shield me from further blows. The entire left side of her head was swollen, her thumb was dislocated, and she had two broken ribs. They made both of us stay overnight in the hospital. Their report must have gone to a high place because within a month we were back in the U.S. living temporarily with Granny.

My mother had a successful teaching career and a reasonable social life but she never remarried. Nor did we ever hear from LEE Roy or about him after the divorce. It's likely he ended up in jail or worse because he was so angry and his anger affected his judgment. It kept him from understanding things in life, large and small. Among the many things he misunderstood was me. Like when he said 'put all that baseball shit behind you' he didn't have the vaguest idea that he was suggesting the impossible. Baseball was in my blood.

I played in high school and junior college and worked for thirty-three years as a major league umpire. I even made it to a real World Series. I am proud of that, of course, but thinking back to when I was twelve and how pure the game was for us at that age and how completely I loved it, I think I would rather have played in the Little League World Series, than have officiated in the major league Series. No kidding, that's the truth.

VENDETTA

More than fifty years ago, a stranger came to my grandparents' house in Key West late one afternoon and knocked on the screen door. I was then ten years old and home alone. I went to the door and looked up at the person, but the sun at that moment was directly behind him. I shielded my eyes and tried to look straight at him, but the sun was too bright, and his face was cast in shadow. Now, all these years later, knowing what I do, it seems fitting that the faceless form I saw that afternoon, framed in a screen door, is my most lasting impression of the man who claimed to be my father and whom I never saw again.

His first words to me were: "Hey, Son, I'm Maynard Bandy."

"Hello," I said, squinting at him.

"Are you Rupert?"

I nodded.

"I'm your Paw, boy, and you're my son." His voice cracked and he nervously picked up a pebble from the ground and tossed it away. Then, as if to be certain he said, "Your last name's Bandy, ain't it?"

I nodded again.

"Pretty much seals the deal," he said. "You *are* my son." As he spoke, he reached out and tried to pull the screen door open, but it was latched. When he did that, I saw him briefly. He looked tired and his overalls were too big for him.

"I can't let you in, Mister. My Mama said so. It's one of the rules when I'm home alone."

"Just wanted to shake hands, Son, but you're doin right by Mazie," he said. "You doin good at school too? Got a good teacher?" We talked about school for a while then fell silent. Finally, Mr. Bandy said, "How'd you like to go get a soda or an ice cream?"

"I can't. That's another rule," I said.

"Well, Son, I figure it's time fer me to be goin then. Was nice to meet you, really. You're a fine lookin boy." I watched him through the screen as he walked slowly back to his pickup. He turned and waved at me twice and just before he slid into the truck he shouted, "Take care, ya hear?"

When my Mama came home from work and I told her Maynard Bandy had come to visit me, she just stood there with her jaw hanging down. Since she didn't say anything, I asked her right away if he really was my father and she shouted, "Yes, and don't you ever ask me that again!" That was the first time I had asked her about him and first time she had yelled at me, ever. She didn't eat any supper that evening and went to bed early without saying good night to me or her Mama and Daddy. The next morning she came downstairs cool and collected and explained that she had married Maynard in high school, he was a musician, and he had chosen a life on the road instead of a life with us. Lastly, she told me in no uncertain terms she didn't want to talk about him again and we didn't until Mama was dying and I was nearly twenty-five.

I thought about him often though because, despite what Maynard and Mama said, I couldn't shake the feeling

that he was not my father. We certainly didn't look alike. Maynard was dark skinned, had black hair and brown eyes, and I was a redhead with blue eyes. Moreover, I had no feeling of kinship for him.

About a year after meeting Maynard, I was awakened late one night by my grandparents, J.T. and Ella Chambliss. They had left their bedroom door open and were arguing about their daughter Mazie, who got pregnant with me when she was eighteen. J.T. was saying it drove him crazy that Mazie still refused to tell him who the father of her child was. At first I thought I was dreaming because the comment made no sense: we all knew it was Maynard Bandy. Mama and I were carrying his family name, after all. Then J.T. rolled out his theory that Mazie had been raped, which was something I didn't know about at my age, but I sensed it was important because Ella became quite upset.

"Let's just back away from this discussion right now," she said. "If you start on this again I won't be able to sleep."

J.T. took her point, but he apparently needed the last word because he added, "You can bet your last buck, Ella, if I ever find out who he is, I'll kill the sonovabitch." This threat made goose bumps stand up on my neck because J.T. had killed before and I had no doubt he could do it again.

"Well, I'm glad you don't know who he is then," Ella shot back in a shaky voice, "because that's exactly what I'd be afraid of." Then she paused. I waited and listened. Finally, Ella said in a voice no longer shaky, "I love you, J.T., more than you know, but I couldn't live with you if I

knew you had murdered someone. I would leave you if you did. Have no doubt." From my perspective, that was the ultimate threat. I didn't want to move away; I didn't want them to divorce; and I was deathly afraid I'd end up in an orphanage.

I lived with this confusion over my identity through my childhood, my adolescence, and into my early adult years. I could see no way to resolve it. Maynard's name was forbidden in our house because he had left Mama and me. It was such a touchy subject I didn't dare ask anyone who knew. And so, I grew up as Maynard Bandy's son while believing I wasn't and wondering who I really was.

Fortunately my granddad, J.T., provided me stability and a role model. I loved him and I knew he loved me, but he was a hard man. He had spent four years as a Marine infantry officer in the Pacific and returned a genuine hero with medals, a crippled leg, and a head full of nightmares. I never heard him talk about those years, but while looking for something in the garage once, I came across the citations that described what he did to earn his medals. Several times when I was alone in the house, I went out to the garage and reread them. I won't go into detail except to say he risked his life over and over again and killed many Japanese soldiers to protect his own men. It's no wonder he still had trouble sleeping. Ella said he had mellowed some since his discharge twelve years ago, but not much. He was one tough guy whose demeanor encouraged obedience and whose standards were high and non-negotiable.

He owned Chambliss Marina, a boat repair facility in the Key West Bight, and had instilled in his workforce the

same esprit and dedication he had instilled in his Marines. He was a man of few words and no bullshit, but his employees stayed with him and the business had begun to turn a nice profit. This did not affect J.T.'s appearance or lifestyle though. He stayed fit by working out hard every day. I once saw him take a hundred bucks off a salesman who bet him he couldn't do one hundred push-ups in three minutes. He preferred beer to liquor or wine, staying home to going out, and t-shirts and shorts year round. His only flamboyant attribute was his IQ, which he tried to hide with his questionable grammar and south Florida accent, but the men knew he was smart. He had a Masters in Mechanical Engineering from Georgia Tech and a solution every time they came to him with a problem they could not solve.

Despite all he did for me, the missing generation between us left a gap that reminded me I didn't have a father to sit in a boat with me on a warm afternoon, reeling in a few fish, and discussing things; I couldn't look up to see my father clapping for me at my baseball games. J.T. was a loyal, protective presence in my life, but he didn't engage in long, intimate conversations with me, or probably with anyone. When I touched on topics that were still too personal or close to his time in the Pacific, I felt his warnings and backed off. Probably everyone did.

As I rollercoastered through adolescence, thoughts of my real father faded. When they did come to mind, I just tossed them aside. In college, when I was pretending to be an intellectual, I read some books on the complex relationship between sons and fathers that made me wonder why I wanted to meet him at all. My answers

seemed to depend on my mood or the last article I had read, but I knew I was gradually moving toward an acceptance of the fact that he would be a permanent disappointment to me. How could I not be disappointed in a man who never showed the courage or the courtesy to face me and give me some answers?

That was my father issue. Mazie was my mother issue. With her tawny hair and dark brown eyes, her delicate long limbs and neck, she reminded me of a fawn, always alert and ready to bolt at the first whiff of danger. Actually, she did bolt once before I was born. She jumped aboard a Greyhound bus and went to Miami without telling anyone. When she finally called to check in, J.T. and Ella pleaded with her to come home, but legally they could not force her to do so. In the end, she stayed quite a long time because someone there was promising to put her in the movies. That didn't happen, of course, and she eventually did come home but she had changed, according to Auntie Bea, my mama's older sister. Mazie had become so anxious and skittish that she had difficulty concentrating and was forgetful. After my birth, Ella and Aunt Bea worried that these traits were not ideal in the mother of a newborn so I became a family care project for the first years of my life, but I was lucky. Auntie Bea loved me without limits from my first day on earth, and as time passed she assumed more and more responsibility for my upbringing.

Bea was born in 1942, just after J.T. left for the Pacific and was four when the war ended and he returned. Although J.T. had seen her only twice during those years, she was much like him, smart, determined and independent. She was a child who never worried her

parents. She sailed through high school with excellent grades, then earned both her Bachelor's and Masters' degrees in architecture from the University of Florida. While looking for work after graduation she had a minor bike collision with a high school classmate, Nappy Broward, a handsome, happy lad who had been a star athlete in high school and later joined the Key West Police Department. Six months later they were married. Bea was thoroughly content with her life until the evening of their fourth anniversary when Nappy was hit and killed by a drunk driver. In true conch fashion, the City gave Bea a job-for-life as its Director of Historical Preservation, but for a long time Bea could summon little interest in life, much less in work. Then, according to Ella, when I was born, Bea's melancholy began to lift. J.T. started calling her Auntie Bea and she began cautiously to reenter the flow of life, not as the carefree girl who had married Nappy, but as a mature, strong woman in need of someone to love. Lucky for me, I was that someone.

Bea loved to tell the story of the first time she saw me. "I went to visit him the day he was born," she would begin, "and I just knew I was here on Earth to love and protect him. I stood behind a glass partition in the hospital and looked at him for seven days, trying to figure how such a small person could touch me so deeply. All's I know was that he did and still does," she would say flushing slightly.

During my first years, Bea would walk over from her office to give me my noon feedings. I have heard folks say that most days she would return to City Hall with Pabulum or green Jell-O in her hair and a spring in her step. Ella said she thought the more time Bea spent with me the

happier she was. She began coming over for evening feedings, after which she would gather me in her arms and ease herself into the same chair Ella used to rock Mazie to sleep. She would push off with her toes, back and forth, back and forth, while the creaky floor sang beneath us.

But Bea was not simply a softy who spent her time feeding me and rocking me to sleep. In fact, as a young girl and teenager, she was quite a tomboy. She followed her father around imitating his every move and they often did things together that were not traditional father-daughter activities. Bea told me J.T. started taking her to the pistol range when she was ten years old. He not only taught her how to shoot, but how to break down each of his pistols, oil them, and put them back together. By the time I was going to the range with them, Bea was an even better marksman than J.T. He was proud of her ability on the range, but he admired her even more for her willingness to fight for what she believed in. The first time she felt the sting of sexism, she fought back hard. Her high school principal had written her a note rejecting her request to take a course in shop because she was a girl. She was sixteen and came to Ella in tears. At dinner that night her parents told her, "Don't cry about it, fight him." And she did. She used the principal's own note – and J.T. quietly called a couple of his press pals – to win overwhelming public support for her request, which forced the principal to reconsider. She studied small gasoline engines in shop that year.

By the time I entered school, Bea was my *de facto* mom. Of course Mazie, J.T. and Ella were constants in my life too, but Bea was the one who taught me to read, swim,

sail and shoot a pistol. She did my laundry and introduced me to ice cream. On my eleventh birthday she met me walking home from school. Without explanation, she walked me into her house, asked me to close my eyes, and led me into a room. "Surprise!" she said and I opened my eyes to find she had converted her study into a bedroom for me. It had everything a boy needed: a big closet, a desk and a lamp with an adjustable neck, a picture of the 1980 Florida Gators, my favorite team, and a cabinet with inside lighting to display my glass animal collection. From that moment I had two homes and I stopped worrying about going to an orphanage.

We all worried about Mama though. She had gradually relinquished her maternal responsibilities to Bea, but she wanted to be included in decisions about me and occasionally reminded Bea that I was *her* son. Bea, who was part of the problem and part of the solution, usually handled these situations deftly, as she did the day she gave me my own bedroom. Mama saw this as an attempt to lure me away from my grandparents' house but Bea preempted a serious fuss by suggesting we go to Miami so Mama could look for a used car. This had long been one of her fondest aspirations so she jumped at the chance.

~~~

Several days later we headed east in darkness. As daybreak approached, the blue-black sky faded to pearl grey, the stars withdrew, and a silver sheen spread across the dark waters of the Atlantic. Moments later, the sun edged above the horizon and threw its beams 30,000 feet into the sky, backlighting the spires of the puffy clouds

gathering on the horizon and turning the heavens a lemon yellow.

Bea told me later that she had been transfixed by what she saw that morning. "I'm not religious," she said in a whisper, "but in the presence of such splendor, I just had to thank God for my many blessings, especially the one in the back seat wearing his Florida Gators baseball hat."

She dropped Mama and me off at the Ford dealership on Flagler Avenue. The Chamblisses had been a Ford family for years because J.T. and the General Manager there were old friends. He bought his pick-up trucks for the Marina there at discounted prices and Bea loved her Mustang convertible. She had called the salesman who sold her the car and arranged for him to take good care of her little sister. "I'll be back in a couple hours," she promised, kissing me on the forehead and waving to her sister.

We turned to face a cement and glass building that looked like a science fiction airport. Mama grabbed my hand and headed directly to the main entrance. She sat me in a metal folding chair and said, "I'm going to go find the salesman who's going to help me. Don't you move a muscle until I come back, hear?"

I sat there for ten minutes watching the green and orange pennants snapping above the lot in the hot Miami wind. Finally, I ran outside to see them up close and as my eyes adjusted to the brightness, they fell upon a low-slung, muscular-looking car that had a chrome search light and chrome strips running from the front fenders to the rear fender skirts. It was silver and to me was as exciting as a rocket ship. I opened the passenger door and climbed in

cautiously, sensing that it was off limits to the public. I crawled across the fragrant red leather seat and knelt behind the steering wheel so I could scan all the gauges like an astronaut would. Then I began the countdown to blast-off.

Ten, nine, eight...I made a *whooshing* blastoff noise, but I shut down the rockets abruptly when the head of a man in a cowboy hat filled the open driver's window. His pale face was so close to mine it startled me. All his blemishes were visible. I saw the squiggly blood vessels that meandered along the sides of his nose. He had a reddish-brown VanDyke beard and a sickishly sweet after-shave scent. When he smiled, which he did during that first eternal moment, it looked painful, like a grimace. But, when I think of him now the first thing that comes to mind are his cold blue eyes. They were hypnotic. When they locked onto my eyes, I could not look away. They were wide set and heavy lidded and their gaze was invasive.

Despite the proximity of our faces neither he nor I withdrew. We remained motionless and communed silently for a few moments. I was oblivious to the sounds and bustle I had noticed earlier. When he reached through the window and patted my thigh, I wasn't frightened or offended.

Then he moved his hand to my crotch. I froze. As I recall, I simply could not move while he fondled me. I don't know how long it lasted but as he withdrew his hand he spoke his first words to me. "I'm Earl Shifflet, Rupert. Wasn't that fun?"

I felt sick. I was so shaken I couldn't speak, but Mr. Shifflet was not waiting for an answer. He was taking in

every feature and expression on my face, every measure of my body. I could feel his eyes crawling all over me like lice and I could see his hand draped directly in front of my chest. I was terrified he was going to lower it to my crotch again. I remember his beautiful white leather coat stitched with swirling dark blue designs and a big chunk of turquoise holding his skinny string tie in place. I concentrated on that stone so I wouldn't cry.

I stole a glance at Mr. Shifflet, hoping to see some sign that he was about to leave, but he startled me again. He had removed his hat to wipe the sweat from his brow and he looked entirely different because he was bald, except for the light red stubble that marched across the back of his head and merged into his sparse sideburns.

I started to shake. Mr. Shifflet must have sensed that I was near the end of my rope. He tousled my hair as he backed away from the car. Then he came toward me again, leaned close and whispered, "You're dead, kid, if you breathe a word of this to anybody, and I'll know if you do." Then he drew his finger across his throat, turned and walked quickly across the lot and into the building. When he was gone, I leaned out of the window and vomited onto the pavement where he had stood.

I do not remember joining up with Mama and Aunt Bea or much about our trip home. I do remember that on the way I saw three men who looked like Mr. Shifflet. At each sighting, I slammed myself down across the back seat and felt prickles run from my head to my neck. I also remember the ocean shining like molten silver, a harsh, gray sky, heat haze boiling off the highway, and saw grass

shaking fitfully in the hot wind and I recall thinking, 'This is like Hell.'

I don't know what lasting effects Mr. Shifflet's perversion had on me. I told no one about it, but by then I was good at keeping secrets. My health was good and I did well in school, but Shifflet interrupted my sleep occasionally and always in the same way. I would see him in a dream, close-up format only. He appeared to be talking but there was no sound coming from his lips. My vision of him was always in black and white, but as it faded to its conclusion, his VanDyke beard turned bright red and his eyes took on an icy blue color. This weird transformation never failed to wake me and I awoke angry so I was usually unable to go back to sleep right away.

Over time, I learned about Earl Shifflet by researching him in libraries and public records, but I had to dig; he was not a publicity seeker. I determined that he owned a Ford dealership, a beer distributorship, a good deal of real estate, and a movie studio. In attempting to see into Shifflet's murky world, it was often difficult to draw a distinction between fact and fiction. Some papers described him as the kingpin of south Florida vice and linked him to a murder-for-hire syndicate; others were more circumspect, possibly due to fear or lack of evidence. Despite numerous run-ins with the law, he had never been charged with a crime. His lawyers certainly knew where the skeletons lay and how to use them.

~~~

Life rolled on. I studied hard and followed in my granddad's footsteps to Georgia Tech. J.T. had built his business into the biggest boat repair facility in the Keys

199

and told me he would rather give the business to me than sell it. So, after completing my Masters in Mechanical Engineering, I started working fulltime as J.T.'s understudy. Ella, who had dabbled in writing children's stories while teaching second grade, had a book published that did well on the national best seller lists. Bea became influential statewide in historical preservation matters and we heard that Maynard Bandy had gone to Nashville to seek his fortune. My Mama drifted away mentally and died in her early forties.

She was bed-ridden her last months and became so thin that as she lay sunk in her mattress you could hardly see her little body beneath the sheet and blanket. She was lucid, though, part of the time. One morning when I was coaxing her to eat, she apologized for being an inadequate mother.

"Mama," I said, "I love you. I don't think of you as inadequate at all." She was making amends and tying up loose ends and it wasn't difficult for me to be charitable. "May I ask you a question now?" I asked, thinking charity might beget honesty.

"Of course you may, Sweetie."

"Was Maynard Bandy really my father?"

She answered so quickly it was as if she had anticipated the question. "No," she said, looking away, "he wasn't. I'm sorry, Rupe, for that too. I bet it's a sin to lie about such an important thing." She seemed to contemplate her own statement before saying, "I'm sorry I did it, but I'd do it again even knowing how difficult it has been to live with the my decision."

"But why did you do it?" I asked.

"Because it was best for you, Rupie. That was my reason for doing everything I did."

"Best for me? You mean going through life believing some innocent guitar player who came to see me only once was my father? Do you mean that's better than knowing who my father really is?" I asked cynically.

"Much, much better," she said.

"You're not going to tell me who he is, are you?" She shook her head back and forth repeatedly. I didn't have the heart to press her further. "That's okay, Mama," I said. I wish I had given her a kiss then, but years of distance interfered.

A week later, J.T. and Ella entered my room at Bea's at 6 a.m. and sat down on my bed. I knew why they were there. Ella put her hand on my shoulder and said, "Rupe, your Mama left us last night. I'm sorry."

J.T. bent down and kissed me on the forehead. He had never kissed me before. "Sorry, Lad," he whispered.

~~~

After Mama's funeral, we all settled into our routines again. The next Sunday morning my grandparents and I were drinking coffee and reading the Sunday papers around their kitchen table. That handsome piece of furniture had borne witness to all the important family discussions in my lifetime and was about to do so again. After my talk with Mama, I had decided to try to confirm what she had told me about Maynard. It was too important to accept at face value.

"We gotta talk, Granddad," I said without preamble.

"What can I do for you, Rupe?" J.T. said.

"I'd like to know who my father is." I could have slipped into the conversation more gracefully, but J.T. was a man of few words and he had taught me well.

It seemed like an hour passed before he said, "So would I, Son, but you ought to leave that alone. No good'll come of it."

"I'm the one to decide that," I said, again sounding sharper than I intended. "I'm twenty-five and I'll be independent and working for a living soon. If my father is alive, it's for me to decide what to do about him."

"You sound like your Mama talking, Son." Then he looked me straight in the eye and said, "Ella and I don't know who your father is...or was. What's more, we believe your father could damn well have contacted you by now if he was interested in you and we don't want you getting hurt by some shitbird who has no feelings for you. You're right though: it's your decision, not ours."

I wanted to keep the conversation focused on the identity of my father so I didn't comment on his absence from my life. Instead I asked, "If you don't know who he is, does that mean he could be Maynard Bandy?"

"It ain't Maynard," J.T. said.

"How do you know, Granddad? How can you be sure?"

"Your mother told us it wasn't Maynard and I checked. He was in jail when she got pregnant."

"But I'm carrying his name, for Pete's sake! Why was I told repeatedly that he was my father if he wasn't?"

Ella jumped into the discussion wiping a tear away. "I want to explain it, J.T., because it was my idea. Rupe, baby, please listen to me with an open mind. You don't remember this, but twenty-five years ago on this little

island, illegitimate children and unwed mothers were not welcome. They were ridiculed and often run out of town."

"I had a classmate named Delores Rhody, Rupe," J.T. interceded. "We were in the same elementary and junior high classes so I knew her well. She got pregnant in the ninth grade, left a pathetic little note, and hanged herself in her backyard. Mazie was depressed when she got pregnant and she had something called anxiety disorder. The doctor told us it was a worrisome combination. We watched her very closely for months because we thought she might do what Delores did," J.T. said.

"We figured the best way we had of preserving Mazie's reputation was to make sure her husband believed he was the father. If Maynard had doubts – and he was a distrustful soul – others would too. And, if rumors started, we feared she might take you and run away, or take her own life." Ella paused, bit her bottom lip. "She and I talked it out right here at this table. I told her, 'Honey child, if you still have kindly feelings toward Maynard, spending a night with him might be a damned sight better than hearing ugly comments about your baby for a long time to come.'" J.T. reached over and took Ella's hand, hoping she would stop, but she couldn't yet. "I didn't need to know they went to the Southernmost Motel, but I sure felt better when she told me Maynard was pleased to be a father. I'm ashamed too, Rupe, for what I suggested, I really am. But to be absolutely honest, you know, I would have done worse things to protect you and Mazie from humiliation and shame."

"Jesus God," was all I could say. We all sat avoiding eye contact for a spell, but there was more business to

attend to so I pressed on. "Okay," I get it, I said, "but why did she refuse to tell me who my father is. Why? I don't get that."

"I've thought about that question every day," J.T. said. "I believe it boils down to two possibilities: shame or fear. My little girl was either so ashamed of what she did or so afraid of what the father would do if she divulged his name that she went to her Maker protecting that secret." J.T. swallowed hard. "I'm an old fart now, but I ain't dead and I'd love to have ten minutes alone with that bastard."

Ella did not take the bait but shot him a nasty glance. The old vendetta argument was still alive. "Rupe, my love," she said standing up, "we have tried to do our best for you all your life. I hope you won't judge us based on this one decision." She looked at me and opened her arms. I walked to her and she folded them around me. That night I went to B.O.'s Fish Wagon, a ramshackle bar on the water, and had a beer or two more than usual.

~~~

J.T. and Ella left on vacation the following day. I told them I would spend the nights at their house for safety's sake. My first night there, as I headed for a cold beer after work, I found a note from Bea on the kitchen counter. It said,

"R, gotta see you sometime. Pls call. Love, B."

I called her right away and said, "I have excellent leftovers. Come on over."

At fifty-two, Bea had a trim figure, played excellent tennis, and looked ten years younger than her age. But that evening when she walked into the kitchen with a

bottle of chilled wine, she looked at least her age and was obviously preoccupied.

"What's up, Beatrice?" I asked giving her a peck on the cheek.

"Let's eat first," she said. We heated the leftovers and had a couple glasses of wine, but she did not eat much. I was still processing the information from J.T. and Ella, but I felt relieved to know the secret that had been lodged between them and me for so long was out in the open. The healing could begin, I thought. Little did I know.

"I have some information for you," Bea said tentatively.

"About what?"

"About your father." She read the expression on my face and said, "Sorry, Rupe. I've been so nervous about this moment. I didn't know how to begin."

"What's the info?" I asked, trying to act calm. Still she hesitated.

"Look," I continued, "you know better than anyone in the world how often I have wondered who he is, what he's like, what I'd be like if he'd been around. Please, Bea."

"Okay, here goes." She took a deep breath. "When you were about eleven I took your mother to Miami to buy a car and you came with us. Maybe you remember that trip."

"Yes, I remember it," I said, nodding.

Bea reminded me that she dropped Mazie and me at the car dealership and set out to visit a friend. Due to a misunderstanding, Mazie's friend was not home, so Mazie returned to the dealership with almost an hour to spare. To pass the time, Bea said, she sat in the grand showroom and people watched; she looked at the shiny new Ford

205

models on display; she wandered the lots outside, all the time keeping an eye out for us. Then, in front of the corporate offices, she spotted a trophy wall laden with newspaper articles, photos, and memorabilia. As she scanned the material, her eyes happened upon a photo of two men shaking hands. She read the caption: "Movie Director Angelino Labriola and Miami Film Studios President Mr. E. Rupert Shifflet discuss a venture at the Fontainebleau Hotel."

"Oh, shit!" I said aloud. It was my worst nightmare, and yet I was awake, sitting in my grandparents' kitchen. Bea had stopped talking. She was looking at me.

"It's Earl Shifflet?" I asked in a whisper.

She nodded. We sat and stared at each other. "I'm sorry, Rupe," she said at last. When I saw that middle name..."

"Me too," I interrupted.

"Yeah, the middle name and the movie studio. I had no idea Shifflet had a movie studio but...sonofabitch." Suddenly tears of rage were running down Bea's cheeks and her face was turning red. I reached out and put my hand on hers. I felt my face go warm too as a volcano of anger welled up in me.

"Are you absolutely positive about this, Bea?"

"I'm sure. I invited Mazie to dinner the next night and she confirmed my fears."

"How did she react when you said his name? I asked.

"She was frightened, really scared!"

"Why was that?"

"Because she thought Shifflet might kill you – and her. Remember, Mazie was only seventeen then when you were

born. If his affair with a minor had been discovered, he could have been prosecuted for statutory rape, consensual or not. Imagine how much more difficult it would have been to prosecute that case if you and Mazie were dead."

"No wonder she never told anybody," I said, aghast.

"Except me," Bea pointed out. "She considered it safer to tell me everything so I would appreciate the danger and keep the secret rather than to keep me in the dark and risk my talking about it."

"But she fell for such a jerk!"

"She was an impressionable teenager, my dear, and he treated her well," Bea explained, instinctively defending her little sister. "He took her to popular night spots, provided her an apartment on South Beach, and talked of making her a movie star. I asked her outright if she knew of Shifflet's reputation and she said, 'No idea, Sister! I was seventeen! What would I know about vice and corruption?' She thought his only business was the film studio," Bea said. Bea thought for a moment. "You know, she spoke of Shifflet as if she really liked him – and probably was naïve enough to think he actually had some affection for her – until she told him she was pregnant."

"Why? What did he do then?"

"He turned on her like the animal he is. She told me he hit her and knocked her to the floor. Gave her a gash on the head that needed stitches. Then he whispered in her ear, 'You are dead to me, Bitch, and your baby is dead too if you ever breathe a word of this to anyone ... and I'll know it if you do.' Then he yelled, 'Get out!' Now you know why she didn't tell Daddy, right? Can you imagine what he

would have done if he'd heard about that little tantrum?"
Bea asked.

"Yeah, I can imagine alright," I said absentmindedly,
but my thoughts were carrying me back to my own
horrendous morning with Shifflet. I had kept those
memories locked away, but they broke out when I heard
what he did to Mama. I remembered the hand on me, the
sickeningly sweet smell of his aftershave, his grimace, and
then I thought of my mother ..."

"This goes to show you his temper and how dangerous
he is." Bea was saying. "I know this must just fill you with
rage, Rupe ..."

"No you don't!" I cut her off and stood, aware that my
voice didn't sound like mine. "You don't have any idea how
it makes me feel." Bea stared at me. "That bastard
molested me when I was eleven years old ... when we went
up there together." I felt faint so I bent over and put my
hands on my knees. "He said I'd be dead if I told anyone."
Bea came over and put her hand on my back.

"Oh, my God! I'm so sorry, Rupie," she said several
times. "I'm so sorry I didn't notice you had been hurt ...
didn't do anything to help you understand it wasn't your
fault." An instant later, she screamed violently at her
anger. I reached out and took her wrists. She tried to tear
herself away from me, but I held onto her for fear she
would injure herself. I held tightly to her wrists and tried
to reassure her gently until the tantrum passed. When it
did, I turned her loose and sat down next to her shaking
and sweaty. It seemed like several minutes passed before
either of us spoke.

"We'll find a good counselor for you to talk to if you want some professional guidance," she said calmly. "Anything you want, Rupie," she said. "Anything."

"Are you okay?" I asked.

"No, I am filled with hatred now, but your secret is safe with me and my best advice: Let's you and me keep it as safe as your Mama did."

My own father had molested me. Jesus! There was so much to think about I didn't know where to start. Bea offered to stay the night, but I wanted to be alone. I needed solitude to clear my head. I walked her home along the quiet sidewalks, asked her if she wanted me to stay with her, and gave her a hug. When I returned, I was tempted to pour myself a shot or two of J.T.'s Laphroaig Scotch, but I collapsed instead onto a lounge chair on the dock and lay there exhausted, listening to the music of the mini-waves lapping on shore and savoring the touch of the soft, tropical air.

As I lay there and felt the stress slightly loosen its grip on my neck and shoulders, I realized my mind had been working on its own: Mama had been right to keep the truth about Earl Shifflet from me. She had been right also to keep his identity a secret – even to the point of taking it to her grave. Earl Shifflet was a psychopath and Mama had sacrificed a normal life and much more to shelter me from him. I owed her so much for that. I owed her revenge.

I was so exhausted that these dark thoughts blew away like smoke on a windy day as soon as my head hit the pillow. I awoke at 7 a.m. with those same thoughts eating their way into my conscience, but I had to go to work. J.T. put me in charge, at least nominally, when he was gone.

While waiting for my coffee at the Five Brothers, I had an epiphany: I could not discuss this with anyone. If I did and were charged with murder later, anyone who had discussed it with me could be found guilty of conspiracy to commit murder. I was alone, contemplating murder, a circumstance so alien to me I felt as if I had drifted outside myself.

~~~

I met J.T. and Ella at the airport that afternoon and before they had put their bags in the trunk Ella said, "Rupie, you look tired. Are you okay?"

"One hundred percent," I said, although that was far from the truth. In fact, I was stymied. I had been thinking about striking back at Shifflet throughout their vacation, but had come up with no workable ideas, much less a plan. I had discarded the thought of going to the police because I couldn't envision how a case could be made against him. His offenses against Mazie and me occurred without witnesses and long ago. Only the effects of his repulsive deeds remained raw and current.

I had visited Shifflet's dealership while they were away, hoping to learn or see something there that would spark my imagination. The salesman who greeted me was a garrulous fellow so I was able to divert our conversation temporarily from my alleged need for a car to his job and then to Shifflet. "Do you want to meet him?" he asked enthusiastically. "He likes to meet customers. He's here today – just saw him."

"No, no. I don't have much time this morning." I said. "Next time maybe. He's got quite a reputation."

"Yeah, I've heard all the rumors," the salesman said. "Tell you what, if you buy a car from me, I'll introduce him to you. You can ask him about his reputation yourself," he said with a wink. Eventually he got down to business and tried to sell me a car and I tried to appear interested but not quite ready to buy. I asked for his card and promised I'd contact him soon.

The salesman's offer to introduce me to Shifflet made me face the fact that I could probably get close enough to shoot him. The question was: if I were close enough to shoot, would I? Could I gun this monster down in cold blood? The moment of truth was drawing near.

The next day I went for a swim after work, as usual. I dove off the dock, swam underwater as far as I could. As I broke the surface and sucked in that first lung-full of sweet, sea air I knew I could not kill him. I knew revenge would not be sweet enough to warrant betting my wonderful life against death in the gas chamber, and I knew that my life for his would be a stupid exchange. Maybe I had known these things all along and had denied them because I wanted so much to make that man pay for all the years he made Mama suffer. Maybe I denied them because deep down I wanted to show I was as brave as my grandfather had been during the war. But, I knew that evening as I swam back to the dock that I was not my grandfather and the two situations were far from equivalent.

Having acknowledged that I could not kill Shifflet myself, I found I couldn't just dump this mess in J.T.'s lap either. He was almost seventy, had a bad leg and a heart problem he didn't talk about. If I told him what Shifflet

had done to Mazie and me, it would have been the same as urging him to go out and get even for us. His pride would have compelled him to try, and in doing so, he would have been risking the good life he had built for himself and all of his family and all of our futures. The final answer was clear: Shifflet was not worth any risk to our family.

And so I found myself in the same position my Mama had been in: Shifflet's threat to kill me followed me around like the menace of a bad disease, but I was neither willing nor able to eliminate that threat. Just like my Mama had been, I was frustrated, even shamed by our bad luck, and yet we had each decided to live with it because we realized it was better than the alternatives.

~~~

I awoke in my own bedroom that unforgettable morning fifty years ago to the coos of mourning doves and the rustling of palm fronds. I padded to the kitchen to make my Cuban *café con leche.* Bea usually made our coffee while she puttered in the kitchen in the early morning, but she had left a note for me the previous afternoon saying she was going to babysit Kat Dannenberg, her goddaughter, and might spend the night there if her parents stayed out late. With her note in hand and clad only in my boxer shorts, I went out the front door and down the porch steps to retrieve the <u>Miami Herald</u> from under the jasmine hedge. I slipped it out of its plastic sleeve, unfolded it, and stood suddenly paralyzed by the headline: "Mob Boss Slain At Home." I stared at a gruesome picture of Shifflet's body splayed out on a flagstone path in his front yard. I don't think I moved again until I finished reading the three-column article. It

sounded as if it were written by an experienced homicide reporter who, based on the trajectories of the fatal .45 caliber slugs, suggested Shifflet had been "assassinated by a professional." One bullet had entered at the top right side of his skull, plowed across both hemispheres of the brain, and exited his ear. The other had entered the back of his head and exited the windpipe. The obituary described Shifflet as "a shadowy figure," who had been implicated, but never prosecuted, in two mob slayings and was known to have been close to Medellin drug lord Pablo Escobar in the 1980's.

When my mind returned to the present, I thought of Bea, the only person who knew of my connection to Shifflet, so I grabbed the phone and called the Dannenbergs'. Rob answered.

"She's not here, Rupe."

"Did she babysit for Kat last night?" I asked.

"Nope. She babysat Thursday, night before last, so we could play *bocce*. Is everything okay?"

"Oh yeah. No problem. I guess I confused one night for the other."

Bea walked in the front door thirty minutes later.

"Hey, good morning, Beatrice," I said. "You got an early start today!"

"Didn't you see my note?"

"No," I lied spontaneously. I had never lied to Bea. I was shocked that I had just done so, but I had just begun to think the unthinkable and I knew, as one knows in a chess match, that her next move, her answer, could checkmate her. I felt sick with anxiety as I endured that interminable second before she replied.

"I've been at the Dannenbergs'," she said, and my heart sank. "Stayed over because they got home so late." I believed Bea had never lied to me either and she didn't do it well. She looked at me, but only briefly. The color drained from her face. "I've got to freshen up and you have to go to the Marina, don't you?"

"Have you seen the <u>Herald</u> today?" I asked. "You should check out the front page before you freshen up." I gestured at the paper on the kitchen table and suddenly felt great sympathy for her. She knew what was coming. She placed her hands palms down on the table on either side of the paper, a four-point stance to steady herself, and bent over it so her head was directly above the headline and a photo of Shifflet. She looked at it, closed her eyes, and gasped. Her legs gave out just as I reached her side and helped her to the sofa. I sat next to her, held her hand, and waited for her to regain control. Finally, she sighed deeply and said, "It was so easy to do."

"*Shhhhhh.* It's just you and me, Bea. No one else will ever know."

Thank you for reading.
Please review this book. Reviews help others find
Absolutely Amazing eBooks and inspire us to keep
providing these marvelous tales.

If you would like to be put on our email list to receive
updates on new releases, contests, and promotions, please
go to AbsolutelyAmazingEbooks.com and sign up.